PAULO FREIRE
AND THE CURRICULUM

Series in Critical Narrative

Donaldo Macedo, Series Editor
University of Massachusetts Boston

NOW IN PRINT

The Hegemony of English
  by Donaldo Macedo, Bessie Dendrinos, and
    Panayota Gounari (2003)
Letters from Lexington: Reflections on Propaganda
  New Updated Edition
  by Noam Chomsky (2004)
Pedagogy of Indignation
  by Paulo Freire (2004)
Howard Zinn on Democratic Education
  by Howard Zinn, with Donaldo Macedo (2005)
How Children Learn: Getting Beyond the Deficit Myth
  by Terese Fayden (2005)
The Globalization of Racism
  edited by Donaldo Macedo and Panayota Gounari (2006)
Daring to Dream: Toward a Pedagogy of the Unfinished
  by Paulo Freire (2007)
Class in Culture
  by Teresa L. Ebert and Mas'ud Zavarzadeh (2008)
Dear Paulo: Letters from Those Who Dare Teach
  by Sonia Nieto (2008)
Uncommon Sense from the Writings of Howard Zinn (2008)
Paulo Freire and the Curriculum
  by Georgios Grollios (2009)
*Freedom at Work: Language, Professional, and Intellectual
Development in Schools*
  by María E. Torres-Guzmán with Ruth Swinney (2009)

PAULO FREIRE AND THE CURRICULUM

GEORGIOS GROLLIOS

Translated by Niki Gakoudi

Paradigm Publishers
Boulder • London

Copyright © 2009 Paradigm Publishers

Published in the United States by Paradigm Publishers, 3360 Mitchell Lane,
Suite E, Boulder, CO 80301 USA.

Paradigm Publishers is the trade name of Birkenkamp & Company, LLC,
Dean Birkenkamp, President and Publisher.

Library of Congress Cataloging-in-Publication Data

Grollios, Giorgos.
    [Paulo Freire kai to analytiko programma. English]
    Paulo Freire and the curriculum / Georgios Grollios ; translated by Niki
Gakoudi.
        p. cm. — (Series in critical narrative)
    Translated from Greek.
    Includes bibliographical references and index.
    ISBN 978-1-59451-747-1 (hardcover : alk. paper)
    1. Curriculum planning—Political aspects.   2. Curriculum planning—Social
aspects.   3. Curriculum planning—Brazil—São Paulo—History—20th
century.   4. Critical pedagogy.   5. Freire, Paulo, 1921–1997.   I. Title.
    LB2806.15.G7613   2009
    375'.001—dc22

                                                            2009004016

Printed and bound in the United States of America on acid-free paper that
meets the standards of the American National Standard for Permanence of
Paper for Printed Library Materials.

Designed and Typeset by Straight Creek Bookmakers.

13 12 11 10 09   1 2 3 4 5

CONTENTS

FOREWORD

George Grollios's brilliant book *Paulo Freire and the Curriculum* is, by far, one of the most comprehensive analyses of Freire's work in the English language, not only because Grollios situates Freire within the sociocultural context that shaped and guided Freire's intellectual trajectory, but also because Grollios, in turn, invites readers to approach Freire beyond his sociocultural context of Recife in northeast Brazil. This approach helps readers understand the political circumstances of the 1950s and 1960s that were marked by the student revolution in France in 1968 and the backlash to it. By inserting Freire within the historical events and the intellectual perspectives that shaped his leading ideas in a fast-changing world of events and thoughts, Grollios achieves in English what Nita Freire so eloquently and rigorously captures in Portuguese: the essence of the humble man from northeast Brazil turned world renowned citizen and intellectual. Freire himself demonstrated this understanding when he argued that "before becoming a world, I was first a citizen of Recife from where I left my backyard in the Yellow House neighborhood. The more rooted I feel in my locality, the greater the possibility to go beyond my location, making me more worldly. No one becomes local using the universal as a point of departure. The existential road is inversed. I am not a Brazilian before so that I can be from Recife. I am first from Recife, from Pernambuco, from the Northeast Brazil. After, I am Brazilian, Latin American, and world citizen."[1]

Grollios's keen ability to analyze the sociocultural and sociopolitical realities of Freire's location, where he studiously attempted to comprehend oppression as an object of knowledge while simultaneously creating ways to denounce it, provides a very rich context for the multifaceted Freirean reality. The conviviality of the peasants taught him the importance of listening and learning from them. Although the dominant forces reduced the peasants to subhumanity and made them objects of history, Freire understood their reality in a radically different way: "All [human beings] were subjects of history and not merely objects of manipulation and exploitation by the powerful so that those condemned to the [subhuman] world, the wretched of the world would emerge from their condition from which they self-outcast themselves from life (to which they had been relegated by the dominant imposition that made them feel and continue to feel less and unworthy), so they can become active subjects and participants in their communities and have the possibility to transform their societies."[2]

It is Freire's compassion and humility that proved indispensable to his success in the development of his leading ideas. However, his compassion and humility would have been insufficient had he restricted himself to his backyard as a mere citizen of Recife without opening himself to the world, in terms both of geography and of the ideas that emanated from philosophers from distant places in the developed world. Although divergent from the human misery experienced by the peasants of Recife, these geographic and cultural places shared a vital reality in common that transcended geography, race, class, gender, and ethnicity: humanity—a humanity drenched in human history.

However, to develop the tools he needed to reflect critically and engage in praxis, Freire chose to satiate his epistemological curiosity by reading critically important Western thinkers and philosophers. Without this reading, his compassion for the oppressed could have been truncated in indignation or anger while lacking the intellectual channels to create a pedagogy rightly informed by both emotion and cognition, a reality that Freire dichotomized. The intellectual tradition that influenced

Freire's thinking as well as his pedagogy has been documented by noted scholars such as bell hooks, George Grollios, Henry Giroux, Donaldo Macedo, and Stanley Aronowitz. According to Nita Freire, "In his phase of greater maturity, [Freire] was already envisioning an Education for autonomy or Pedagogy of Autonomy, that transcend[ed] the concept [of] emancipation (and consequently the education for emancipation) discussed in his revision of Social Critical Theory. The Emancipation that has its point of departure in Kant, has its roots in Hegel and Marx and achieved its more elaborated expression in the School of Frankfurt [and] goes through Adorno, Horkheimer, Lukács, Marcuse, Dewey, Piaget, and Habermas."[3]

Grollios, along with Giroux and Aronowitz, among other writers, has correctly situated Freire within a rich philosophical tradition—a tradition that is reinvented in his engagement in praxis in his Brazilian location but is not restricted to his location, even though those who resist his leading ideas attempt to limit Freire's success to a Third World context. They do so to dismiss his leading ideas, which pointedly call for the transformation of the world into one in which all people are treated with the respect and dignity that they deserve.

It is also this rich tradition that enabled Freire to break with the instrumentalist and behaviorist vision of curriculum, a rupture that constitutes a significant contribution that remains ill understood by many liberal educators who selectively reduce Freire's leading ideas on curriculum and pedagogy to a method. These educators ignore the fact that Freire always viewed the curriculum as crucial to a school's operation and that he did not hold with a social efficiency perspective on curriculum planning. In addition to ignoring Freire's opposition to curricula intended to reinforce the ideology of and control by the dominant social classes, conservative and many liberal educators refuse engagement with Freire's radical democratic educational proposals by relegating their effectiveness to Third World contexts.

But it can no longer be argued that Freire's pedagogy is appropriate only in Third World contexts. For one thing, we are experiencing a rapid Third Worldization of North America (particularly after the imposition of neoliberal policies) in which inner cities resemble more and more the shantytowns of the Third World, with a high level of unemployment, poverty, violence, illiteracy, human exploitation, homelessness, and human misery. The abandonment of our inner cities and the insidious decay of their infrastructures, including their schools, make it very difficult to maintain the artificial division between the First World and the Third World. It is just as easy to find Third Worldness in the First World inner cities as it is to discover First World opulence in the oligarchies in El Salvador, Guatemala, and many other Third World nations.

The Third Worldization of the North American is also threatening the already anxious middle class with high unemployment, loss of economic status, exponential rise in home foreclosures, and a perpetual fear that one is one paycheck way from class downgrading. That is why during the last presidential campaign both Barack Obama and John McCain kept promising protection for the middle class, even though many sectors targeted for job creation were, in reality, part of the working class. The gradual erasure of the middle class is generating much anger and confusion in a society that falsely and arrogantly (if not stupidly) denies the existence of class, even though the media and politicians are constantly referring to the need to do more for the middle class or are demanding that more attention be paid to the working class given the loss of the U.S. manufacturing base.

What the media, politicians, and the general public will never acknowledge is the existence of the upper and ruling classes because the dominant ideology prefers to hide their blind celebration of a savage capitalism where the asymmetrical distribution of wealth has created a new oligarchy characterized by tycoons and "Park Avenue hedge-fund managers ... [who engage] in clueless extravagance."[4] Alongside this clueless extravagance live billions of people who are condemned to a subhuman survival on two dollars per day—a phenomenon that leads to "the transgressions of a universal human ethic that ought to be considered criminal [but] is [instead] programmed [as] mass unemployment, which leads so many to despair and to a kind of living death."[5]

A significant contribution of this book is the author's audacity in unapologetically critiquing Freireans and "wannabe" Freireans who, due to their class position or assimilation to the dominant white class structure, selectively appropriate aspects of Freire so that they can claim the mantle of progressive educators while retaining the same class privilege that they astutely denounce at the level of discourse. By staying only at the level of discourse, these Freirean verbalists (those who talk a great progressive talk but are betrayed by their secret conservative position) have a penchant for reducing Freire to a methodology—a process through which his leading ideas about social justice and liberation are selectively appropriated so as to paralyze his ever-present challenge to educators to engage in praxis. It is only through praxis, not through infantilizing educational practices, that there can be hope for the transformation of both the social structures that generate human misery and the very actors who construct, shape, and maintain a necrophiliac view of history. That is, by relegating Freire's radical democratic ideas to, for example, the dialogical method, these educators attempt to use their association with Freire as a form of progressive mascot while remaining complicit with a neoliberal worldview that promotes a fatalistic discourse designed to immobilize history so that they can accommodate to the status quo. It is through the status quo that they maintain their privilege and reap benefits; at the same time, they refuse to see the evil of a callous capitalism that has given rise to the robber barons of the twenty-first century, who accumulate a vast store of wealth while the majority of the world's people are dispossessed, exploited, and routinely live in subhuman conditions.

Grollios not only critiques this vulgarization of Freire's work; he also offers a comprehensive analysis of Freire's curriculum, whose goal is the radical democratization of schools—a democratization that "should involve the passage from one mentality to another because it primarily constitutes a way of life, not merely of governing educators would contribute to the birth of the new society by espousing a critical education."[6] Thus, Freire's notion of pedagogy goes beyond methods as he "had little patience with education as either a form of training, method, or as a political and moral practice that closed down history, the potential of individual and social agency, the joy and importance of engaged solidarity, the importance of social responsibility, and the possibility of hope."[7] That is why Freire never hesitated to take on the Herculean task of democratizing the more than seven hundred schools of São Paulo, Brazil—an urban school system beset with all the well-known urban problems, managed in a totalitarian manner, excluding huge segments of lower-class students whose school experience was, at best, alienating and, at worst, dehumanizing. Paulo Freire's notion of educational transformation also involves the democratization of pedagogical and educational power so that students, staff, teachers, educational specialists, and parents come together to develop a grassroots plan that accepts the tensions and contradictions always present in all participatory efforts, thereby searching for a democratic substantivity.[8]

This search for democratic substantivity is evidenced in the transformation of the curriculum so that when one "necessarily [teaches] the content, one teaches also how to think critically."[9] Thus, the transformation of the curriculum requires rigorous analysis that leads to the prioritization of the following goals:

- Democratization and access
- Democratization of administration
- New quality of teaching
- Youth and adult education

In emphasizing and prioritizing the democratization of schools, Freire had to decentralize power so that school-based administrators were divested of excessive power. At the same time, he had to create structures where teachers, students, parents, school staff, and the community could participate and contribute in the school transformation process. As Freire ethically argued, "In a really progressive, democratic, and non-authoritarian way, one does change the 'face' of schools through the central office. One cannot decree that, from today on, the schools will be competent, serious, and joyful. One cannot democratize schools authoritarianly."[10]

Compare the goal of democratizing schools in Brazil, a country that had just begun to experience a fragile democracy after decades of cruel military dictatorship fully supported by the United States, with the proposals put forth by President Obama, cleverly enveloped in empty slogans such as "Change that you can believe in," "Yes, we can," and "the audacity of hope." He rendered these slogans empty by advancing educational proposals predicated on competition, high-stakes testing, linkage of pay to performance, and charter schools, all of which are a manipulation of scarce resources to benefit those who can best compete while abandoning a very large segment of urban students (mostly poor and minority) locked into educational warehouses with little resources, incompetent teachers, and a despairingly inferior education. In essence, Obama's proposals for education adhere to the failed neoliberal policies that have imploded in all sectors of society. These policies have left behind a sea of human misery worldwide and a financial crisis that is getting worse while the architects of neoliberal ideology either are part of Obama's new administration or are managing the same financial institutions that they bankrupted while shamelessly collecting billions of dollars, giving socialism for the rich a more naked meaning.

The financial crisis increasingly appears overwhelming and impossible to contain, given how deeply embedded it is in the underlying political and economic power structures that emerged in the conservative counterrevolution that began with the election of Ronald Reagan in 1980. Moreover, Obama's reforms, particularly his economic and education policies, offer no alternative vision about how to change the underlying values and institutions that shape these important sectors of society. Hence, the financial bailout is led by many people who produced it, and the reforms for education largely echo the same old corporate endorsement of vouchers, privatization, pay for performance, high-stakes testing, union busting, and the deployment of military schools for poor white kids and youth of color.[11]

What is even more disturbing is that the sustained neoliberal attack on the social state and its disinvestment in those political, social, and economic spheres vital to the development of healthy and critically informed citizenry have worked quite successfully in tandem with a new and vicious rationality—produced in countless sites, such as the media and higher education—that constructs adults and young people according to the dictates, values, and needs of a market fundamentalism. All aspects of life are now measured according to the calculations of a philosophy that construes profit-making as the essence of democracy and consuming as the only operable form of citizenship.[12]

Government in this case operates not only within the parameters of a corporate state but also within the principles of a ruthless market, whose spectacle of cruelty can no longer hide behind its appeal to self-interest, freedom, and, least of all, democracy. But simply criticizing the market, the privatization of public goods, the politics of deregulation, and the commercialization of everyday life, while helpful, is not enough. Stirring denunciations of what a neoliberal society does to public institutions, identities, and social relations do not go far enough. What is equally necessary is developing a language that moves beyond both the politics of Obama's so-called postpartisan notion of hope and a growing cynicism that registers not merely the depth of the current economic and political crisis but also the defeatist assumption that power operates exclusively in the service of domination, tyranny, and violence.

Jacques Rancière rightly criticizes this cynical stance with his insistence that "the critique of the market today has become a morose reassessment that, contrary to its stated aims, serves to forestall the emancipation of minds and practices. And it ends up sounding not dissimilar to reactionary discourse. These critics of the market call for subversion only to declare it impossible and to abandon all hope for emancipation."[13] Rancière cannot imagine a mode of criticism or a politics that shuts down resistance, play, and hope—nor should we as teachers, parents, and young people.

At stake here is the need for a new politics of resistance and hope, one that mounts a collective challenge to a ruthless market fundamentalism that for the last thirty years has spearheaded the accumulation of capital and wealth at all costs, the com-modification of young people, and the usurpation of democratic modes of sovereignty. At the center of this struggle is a market sovereignty that has not only replaced the state as the principal regulatory force in developing economies of inequality and power but has also gained legitimacy and strength through modes of education, persuasion, and consent that rely on the force of new media technologies, corporate values, commodified social relations, and a calculating rationality, all of which have to be challenged and transformed. Any politics capable of disabling the sovereignty of the market must clarify in political and pedagogical terms a vision, project, discourse, and set of strategic practices necessary to confront a neoliberal order that views democracy as the enemy and flawed consumers as expendable.

Free-market fundamentalism, or neoliberalism (as it is called in some quarters), has played a major role in creating not only massive human suffering, a financial Katrina, and millions of displaced lives but also a weakened social state and a failing democracy made all the more ominous by the dumbing down of public discourse and the emptying out of critical public spheres. Democracy is about neither the sovereignty of the market nor a form of state governance based largely on fear, manipulation, and deceit. Any attempt at challenging neoliberal sovereignty and the national (in)security state must recognize the need for a politics in which matters of education, power, and governance are mutually determined. Such a challenge, in part, rests on a politics that takes seriously the need to understand not only how the institutions of economic Darwinism emerged and recently came unglued but also how and why modes of governing that embody the grand ideologies of a deflated Gilded Age appealed to so many Americans. Frank Rich is right in alerting us to the importance of analyzing how a bankrupt neoliberalism has given us a "debt-ridden national binge of greed and irresponsibility [partly through] mass forms of conspicuous consumption and entertainment."[14]

Implicit in Rich's argument is the need to rethink the discourse of crisis, complicating its underlying causes by raising questions about the role of media and other educational institutions in celebrating and legitimating the pernicious and corrupting values of a rabid market-driven society eager and determined to high-jack social responsibility, noncommodified public spheres, and meaningful citizenship, while treating with scorn any discourse of compassion, mutual worth, and ethical responsibility. Clearly, one challenge the current crisis offers anyone concerned about the fate of democracy is the need for a thorough understanding of how this legacy of market-driven fundamentalism can be comprehended in terms of its power in shaping subjects, citizens, institutions, culture, values, and particular kinds of actions.

For instance, how is it that the same old values and market-driven fundamentalism used to support taxes for the rich, eliminate the social state, and discredit any commitment to the public good are being mobilized once again by Republicans to thwart Obama's stimulus package without provoking a massive public outcry among either the mainstream media, academics, or the general public? Or, even worse, where is the moral outrage among so many Americans who are suffering from the consequences of a thirty-year rule of neoliberal policies aimed at waging a war on the welfare state, science, dissent, the environment, workers, young people, and all aspects of the public good? Democratic politics and the struggles informed by such a politics cannot come about without putting into place these spaces, spheres, and modes of education that enable people to realize that in a real democracy power has to be responsive to the needs, hopes, and desires of its citizens and other inhabitants around the globe.

Democracy is not simply about people wanting to improve their lives; it is more importantly about their willingness to struggle to protect their right to self-determination and self-government in the interest of the common good. Under the reign of free-market fundamentalism, market relations both expanded their control over public space and increasingly defined people as either consuming subjects or commodities, effectively limiting their opportunity to learn how to develop their full range of intellectual and emotional capacities to be critical citizens. Sheldon Wolin has rightly argued that if "democracy is about participating in self-government, its first requirement is a supportive culture of complex beliefs, values, and practices to nurture equality, cooperation, and freedom."[15]

The militarized corporate state and the sovereign market reduce the materiality of democracy to either an overcrowded prison or a shopping mall, both of which are more fitting for a society vulnerable to the winds of totalitarianism. The fundamental institutional and educational conditions that connect social, political, and personal rights to a viable notion of agency have been under attack for the last thirty years and now face a moment of crisis as severe as the current economic crisis.

As education turns to training in the public schools and higher education willingly models itself as a business venture or welcome recipient of Pentagon largesse, corporate culture reigns unchallenged as the most powerful pedagogical force in the country, while "democracy becomes dangerously empty."[16] Unfortunately, Obama seems less than inspiring when it comes to mobilizing a new politics that makes public and higher education central to the struggle for democracy. A visionary politics needs to be willing to enlist and actively mobilize artists, intellectuals, academics, parents, young people, workers, and others in the struggle for a public able and willing to confront through multiple levels of resistance the institutions, policies, and values of an ever-expanding military-industrial and academic complex. Obama's call to put money into rebuilding the infrastructures of schools is to be applauded, but it is largely canceled out by his adherence to an educational policy that views schools less as an investment than as an extension of the market, to be largely driven by the corporate values and accountability schemes that the Bush administration supported. Obama's educational policies need to be pushed in a very different direction, one that is able to recognize the value of critical education for reasons Zygmunt Bauman illuminates with razorlike precision:

Adverse odds may be overwhelming, and yet democratic (or, as Cornelius Castoriadis would say, an autonomous) society knows of no substitute for education and self-education as a means to influence the turn of events that can be squared with its own nature, while that nature cannot be preserved for long without "critical pedagogy"—education sharpening its critical edge, "making society feel guilty" and "stirring things up" through stirring human consciences. The fates of freedom, of democracy that makes it possible while being made possible by it, and of education that breeds dissatisfaction with the level of both freedom and democracy achieved thus far, are inextricably connected and not to be detached from one another. One may view that intimate connection as another specimen of a vicious circle—but it is within that circle that human hopes and the chances of humanity are inscribed, and can be nowhere else.[17]

Making education central to any viable notion of politics as well as making the political more pedagogical suggests that intellectuals, artists, community workers, parents, and others need to connect with diverse groups of people in those public and virtual sites and spheres that not only enable new modes of dialogue to take place but also work to move beyond such exchanges to the much more difficult task of building organized and sustainable social movements. While it is true that anyone who takes politics seriously needs to take into consideration the profound transformations that have taken place in the public sphere, especially those enabled by new technologies, and how such changes can be used to develop new modes of public pedagogy in which young people are provided with the skills, knowledge, interests, and desire to govern themselves, it is simply wrong to suggest that real change only happens online.[18]

Building a more just, ecologically sustainable, and democratic future, or as Jacques Derrida puts it, the promise of "a democracy to come,"[19] demands a politics in which the new technologies are important but only insofar as they are used in the context of bringing people together, reclaiming those public spheres where people can meet, talk, and plan collective actions. We must learn to resist all technologies that reinforce the sense of excessive individualism and privatization at the heart of the neoliberal worldview. We need more than bailouts; we need a politics that reinvents the concept of the social while providing a language of critique and hope forged not in isolation but in collective struggle that takes social responsibility, commitment, and justice seriously.

We live at a time when social bonds are crumbling and institutions that provide collective help are disappearing. Reclaiming these social bonds and the protections of the social state means, in part, developing a new mode of politics and education in which a critically educated public is as central to this struggle as the future of the democratic society it once symbolized. At the heart of this struggle for both young people and adults is the pressing problem of organizing and energizing a vibrant cultural politics to counter the conditions of political apathy, distrust, and social disengagement so pervasive under the politics of neoliberalism. For this we need a new vocabulary that, in part, demands taking back formal education and diverse modes of public pedagogy for democratic purposes while also refashioning social movements and modes of collective resistance that are democratic in nature and global in reach.

Culture in this instance is not merely a resource but an instrument of political power. What must be emphasized in this vision of a democracy to come is that there is no room for a politics animated by a rationality that is about maximizing profit and constructing a society free from the burden of mutual responsibility—that is, a society whose essence is captured in the faces of children facing the terror of a future with little hope of survival. Economic crises do more than throw people out of jobs; they also open up an opportunity for social movements and political demands that serve to educate those in power and push them in a very different direction. This is a moment in which education becomes the foundation not simply for collective change but also for a rewriting of the social contract, an expansion of the meaning of social responsibility, and a renewed struggle to take democracy back from the dark times that have inched us so close to an unimaginable authoritarianism. Instead of accommodating the obscene fundamentalism of the market, we should adhere to Freire's unyielding insistence that "the place upon which a new rebellion should be built is not the ethics of the marketplace with its crass insensitivity to the voice of genuine humanity but the ethics of universal human aspiration. The ethics of human solidarity."[20]

—*Henry Giroux, Panayota Gounari, and Donaldo Macedo*

ACKNOWLEDGMENTS

⊷

Numerous colleagues—teachers of primary, secondary, and higher education, as well as students, both graduate and undergraduate—have encouraged me to write a book about Paulo Freire's pedagogical theory based on the classes I teach at the Department of Elementary Education at the Aristotle University and at the "Dimitris Glinos" Teachers' Training College. Many others, during commemorative lectures, day conferences, and congresses, persuaded me to write on this topic. It is impossible to name everyone who encouraged me here, but I wish to express my heartfelt thanks to each and every one.

I do feel deeply obliged to mention certain colleagues, not only because their thoughts on the writing of this book were similar to mine but also because they helped me by reading and providing valuable comments on first drafts of the manuscript. I refer to Vasilis Alexiou, Charalampos Noutsos, and George Tsiakalos, whose advice was most helpful. I also would like to thank those who helped me with the bibliography: Tasos Liampas, Michalis Batilas, Eleni Drenogianni, and Pavlos Charamis.

A special mention and my sincerest gratitude go to Spyros Rasis, my teacher when I first started pedagogical studies in the 1980s, not only because back then he brought me closer to the theory of Paulo Freire but also because, almost twenty years later, he revealed to me invaluable sources of knowledge and fields of study. In a nutshell, he opened me up to new horizons.

Concerning the innumerable hours involved in writing the book, Xanthi, Dimitris, and Matina yet again openhandedly offered their multifaceted support, and I am unable to express sufficiently my appreciation and indebtedness. For this reason, and because a previous book was dedicated to Xanthi, I dedicate this book as a token of love to Dimitri and Matina.

Panayota Gounari insisted on trying to publish the book in the United States, and she offered me valuable insights and encouragement to make it much better. Niki Gakoudi did excellent work on the translation. Rosemary Carstens provided useful editorial advice, and Jan Kristiansson did thorough copyediting work. I am obliged to thank them all.

Last but not least, I owe special gratitude to Donaldo Macedo and Dean Birkenkamp for their useful recommendations and for their decision to publish my book in the Critical Narrative Series of Paradigm Publishers.

INTRODUCTION

Paulo Freire wrote *Pedagogy of the Oppressed* in 1968–1969 in Chile, while in exile due to the military dictatorship in his country, Brazil. At that time, in 1968, a wave of uprisings was inundating the world. These uprisings shook but did not manage to overthrow capitalism in the developed European countries, such as, France, Germany, and Italy, where the student movement and workers rallies played a leading role. Along the same lines, in the United States in 1968 the civil rights, the student, and the anti–Vietnam War movements also reached a peak.

The events of 1968 did not affect only the developed countries of the West. In Mexico, there were outbreaks with the mass movement and student massacre at the 1968 Olympic Games; in Czechoslovakia there was the short-lived Prague Spring, which ended with the invasion of Soviet troops; and in China there was the Cultural Revolution, which was seen by many as a revolt against the bureaucratization of socialism. The wave of uprisings continued with less intensity in the 1970s, with the anticolonialist and anti-imperialist struggles in Africa and Asia and the fall of totalitarian regimes in southern Europe. Similarly, in Chile the attempt at sociopolitical transformation drowned in blood during the military coup in 1973.

This polymorphous wave brought to the surface, mainly in the developed countries of the West, a series of ideas and demands associated with older revolutionary traditions that the Left had degraded. Among them were denunciation of the alienation that characterized capitalist societies; rejection of dominant power relations in production, in education, and in the family; critique of the division between manual and intellectual labor, technocracy and economism; and deep probing of the struggles that, until then, had gone unrecognized, such as the exploitation and oppression of racial minorities and women, the destruction of the environment, and the industrialization of culture. Finally, there was talk again about direct democracy, liberation, collectivism, and solidarity. These ideas and demands were associated with the dismissal of the social-democratic truce among the social classes that had been established by the welfare state, as well as the rejection of the policies of the pro-Soviet communist parties, which until then were seen by many Leftists as the unerring social architects behind the gradual transformation of the state into a formation commensurate with that of the regimes of Eastern Europe.

Despite the varied ways in which the wave of 1968 took shape in each country, it also comprised a new key element, mainly in the developed countries of the West: it brought certain social groups to the forefront that, in turn, formed temporary alliances with the working class. This phenomenon was the result of particular social changes that had taken place following World War II, such as a shrinking of the rural class and of traditional groups of the middle class; an increase in the number of wage earners among the large urban, especially white-collar workers; and a dramatic rise in the number of university students.

These new social clusters, which were gradually pressured in complex ways by the proletarianization tendencies of their work conditions, expressed a yearning for an antibureaucratic, democratic socialism that was in line with pioneering workers groups. For the first time, students and white-collar workers from the middle classes proceeded to form an anticapitalist and anti-imperialist alliance. Although ephemeral, that alliance still continues to have strategic significance in our days, because it is associated with the potential that exists for establishing a new sociopolitical majority, which will pave the way for a radical societal restructuring with a democratic socialist orientation.

In Chile, Freire came into contact with the spirit of the 1968 uprisings in a very particular manner. Having had his hopes for a democratic reconstruction of Brazil dissipate after the military coup of 1964, he took advantage of the ardent discussions taking place in Chile about Che Guevara and the Cuban revolution, Herbert Marcuse's views on the student movement, and the criticism by the Chinese Cultural Revolution of the bureaucratization of socialism in order to develop a new pedagogy: a pedagogy of the oppressed. A central point of this pedagogy was his particular perspective on curriculum planning, which constitutes the theme of this book. It was formulated in the years 1968–1969 and was enriched with his 1970s experience of implementing this pedagogy in Guinea-Bissau, where he attempted to help build a new socialist society. Freire's perspective on curriculum planning falls within a particular theoretical framework that is characterized by certain elements. Three of these elements are prominent.

First, he approaches pedagogy as a political process: the aims, content, forms, methods, materials, and evaluation, that is, each particular aspect of pedagogic theory and practice, are political. To take a neutral stance vis-à-vis all these components of pedagogy constitutes a political position in itself, which consciously or unconsciously reinforces the dominant social order.

Second, Freire supports an ongoing struggle against a subjective and individualistic approach to empowerment, as well as against a mechanistic-determinist understanding of history as predetermined future. This historical view was projected by both the dominant social classes and dogmatic Marxist factions.

Third, he denounces the exploitative and oppressive capitalist reality while announcing a project for the future of education and society rooted in democratic processes. In addition to promoting socialist ideals, this project combats the false dichotomies between theory and practice, as well as between intellectual labor and manual labor.

At the beginning of the 1980s, the power dynamics among social classes started to shift because the wave of uprisings had failed to overthrow capitalism and the dominant social classes had mounted a systematic ideological and political counterattack in the previous decade. In 1973 the first economic depression since World War II manifested, signaling a transition from the "thirty glorious years" of postwar development to a period of crisis and a neoliberal-neoconservative capitalist reform. There was an indissoluble association between the crisis and this reform because behind the overaccumulation of capital was an evolving correlation of power among social classes that reflected the contradictions inherent in capitalist production. This was why the capitalist nations handled the crisis not by confining themselves to devaluing the insufficiently exploited individual capital but rather by waging open social warfare against the forces of labor.

The dominant social classes realized that the postwar welfare policies had proved useless in preventing a challenge to capitalist economic, social, and political power relations. The neoliberal-neoconservative capitalist reform was, first and foremost, a full-scale attack of the powers of capital at an international level. This reform continues to unfold today, although at a different pace and with particular characteristics from country to country; it aims at a radical change of power dynamics at the expense of the forces of labor. The most important aspects of the neoliberal-neoconservative capitalist reform were, and continue to be, the formation and strengthening of supranational mechanisms, the restriction of the social functions of the state, and changes to the forms of relations of production and organization.

The rise of the New Right in the wake of the 1970s crisis and reform was impressive. From a political standpoint, it expressed a return to basic Western bourgeois political values, such as the naturalness of market forces as opposed to bureaucratic expansion and state economic intervention; the moral superiority of individualism as opposed to collectivism; and the necessity of a powerful state, in the name of law and order, as opposed to a "weak" conception of state rooted in perceptions of social justice. At the beginning of the 1990s, the neoliberal-neoconservative capitalist reform reached its peak of euphoria with the collapse of the Eastern bloc and the Soviet Union, the end of the cold war, and the unification of Germany. The notions of entrepreneurship, competition, and individual freedom appeared undefeatable and inherent in human nature.

However, this peak of optimism very soon began to wane. Despite neoliberal promises, deregulation of the labor market and curbing of the welfare state did not result in full employment, nor did these measures lead to free competition for a large number of businesses. On the contrary, the end result was the mere replacement of monopolies with other corporations, which had the same, if not greater, concentration of economic power. By the end of the first half of the 1990s, not only did the symptoms of the socioeconomic crisis continue to persist, but they also became even more pronounced. There was a sharp rise in unemployment as well as in the number of the poor and homeless, increased immigration, an unleashing of racism, degradation of both the function and authority of the official institutions of parliamentary democracy, and the emergence of and growing support for multifarious nationalisms.

The logic of competition in education did not produce the satisfactory answers to major social problems that had been promised by the dominant rhetoric of the 1980s. The assumption that the solution to these problems could be found in the domain of education, not in socioeconomic and cultural state policies, resulted in a drastic reduction in the number of job positions as well as a marked rise in violence and crime. It was not long before the general consensus on the rationality of neoliberal and neoconservative policies started to crack: in Europe, the workers' movement fought hard battles, and referenda concerning Europe's unification reflected widespread dissatisfaction and protest; in Central and Latin America new radical movements emerged, with the Zapatistas in Mexico being the first.

During the years of conservative "renaissance" and neoliberal dominance, there were intellectuals who, despite having aligned themselves with the wave of dissent in 1968, decided to change track. Some discovered the allurement of "partial" changes and the huge possibilities of new technologies; they wound up praising and/or justifying capitalism. Others went even further, actively supporting imperialistic war operations, which dispelled the myth of world peace that was supposed to have come about with the end of the cold war. In contrast, Freire's reaction was sharply different.

By 1980, the military dictatorship in Brazil had fallen and Freire had returned from exile. In that year he participated in founding the Workers Party, a new political party with a socialist orientation. It was composed mainly of workers, intellectuals, the new middle classes, and young people. The Workers Party played a significant role in democratizing the political life of Brazil, and by the end of the 1980s, it was counting substantial electoral successes, one of which was a victory in the municipal elections of Sao Paulo. Freire was then called on to face a new challenge: the implementation of his perspective on curriculum planning in the official education system of a city with a population of 10 million.

In the interim, Freire had collaborated with critical educators in the United States, such as bell hooks, Donaldo Macedo, Henry Giroux and Ira Shor, who had all been influenced by his pedagogical theory. This collaboration was useful for Freire, because he was able to reexamine his ideas and adapt his positions for the intervention that he was to implement in the official education system of his native country, which in the meantime had developed economically during his exile and in which the neoliberal dogmas had begun to be applied.

Until his death in 1997, Freire continued to support the view that education was not the fundamental institution that shaped society. In fact, he pointed out that education was shaped according to the interests of the dominant classes, whose aim was to systematically reproduce their ideology; however, this shaping was both conflictual and historical. He claimed that an interpretation of the social and educational changes and the factors that determine the limits of pedagogical and political action in each particular conjuncture should be based on the concept of the struggle among the social classes.

The new curriculum based on Freire's perspective was at the core of school reform in Sao Paulo from 1989 to 1992. Despite the short period of the reform's implementation, its positive outcomes included a substantial improvement in school performance and a noticeable reduction in the school dropout rate. In addition, the fact that both teachers and students were actively involved indicated that Freire's perspective on curriculum planning was relevant to the education of illiterate adult peasants in rural areas *and* to the thousands of students of a large, modern, industrial city. In other words, it is erroneous to regard this perspective as something exotic and suitable only for the so-called Third World.

Freire's contribution to curriculum planning, as presented and analyzed in this book, can be studied through the lens of three questions. The first deals with his positions on curriculum planning, the second is devoted to the historical development and the character of his perspective on curriculum planning, and the third refers to his perspective's relationship to others and its contemporary value. To address the third question, we will need to turn to a comparative framework of analysis. In the present study, I will use as my framework for a comparative analysis the perspectives on curriculum planning that appeared during the twentieth century in the United States.[1]

To study Freire's contribution to curriculum planning, I will examine Freire's positions on the goals, the content, the planning process, and the role of the participating subjects. I will examine a broad spectrum of texts written by Freire, define periods in his work, and draw parallels between Freire's positions on curriculum planning in each period and the way these relate to his respective political positions.[2] As for the book's structure, in Chapters 1, 2, and 3 I will examine how economic, social, political, and ideological conditions, primarily in Brazil, but also in other social contexts, resonate with the formation of Freire's positions in each of the three periods of his work (one period per chapter). In Chapter 4, I will conclude with a discussion of the formation and character of his perspective on curriculum planning as well as its differentiation from other perspectives and its contemporary value.

Freire's perspective on curriculum planning should be of interest not only to those specializing in curriculum studies, but also to all educators. Educators face the imposition of curricula on a daily basis, and at the same time they are under pressure to meet curricular goals and succeed in terms of the imposed curricular norm. This process leaves them with little to no space to question forms of the dominant neoconservative and neoliberal ideology now inherent in these curricula. This same process anesthetizes them to the knowledge, skills, and lived experiences that students bring to school, and thus educators refrain from developing forms of critical consciousness in collaboration and in solidarity with their students.

This type of highly standardized curriculum promotes homogenization and standardization of the students' culture, especially through behavioral objectives, conservative values, and the development of limited skills that are designed to meet the needs of businesses/corporations. The main educational goal here is the production of a human capital flexible enough to adapt to the changing labor market and never inclined to challenge the established social order. In the dominant ideology framework, curricula are projected as culturally, ideologically, and politically neutral and connected with a supposedly neutral control system: "good" students will acquire "good" knowledge and will find "good jobs." The neoconservative-neoliberal dogmas have redefined the role of educators as contributing to the smooth functioning of an education in which the logic of commodification and social Darwinism prevail.

Freire's view opposes curricula that represent and express the hegemony of dominant social classes at school. Freire invites educators to understand with more clarity the ways in which educational institutions are structured, as well as the forms of resistance that emerge in educational sites. Based on this understanding, educators can enrich their critique and develop democratic strategies of intervention at school that will call into question capitalism as a natural form of social organization and its equation with democracy, and they will unveil the exploitation and the destruction of natural and social resources on which capitalism thrives. Such strategies will promote students' critical awareness while at the same time enabling them to defend their right to a high-standard public education.

Within this framework, there can be no binarism in the educators' political and pedagogical activities. Democratic strategies of intervention within schools are inextricably connected to political action. Struggles against poverty, unemployment, racism, the shrinking of democratic liberties and human and social rights, as well as struggles for a radical sociopolitical transformation with a socialist direction are part and parcel of the present and the future of education. Educators must find inspiration in these struggles in order to be able to base their practices on respect for the students' knowledge and abilities, to teach in a democratic way by critically analyzing different perspectives, and to help develop their students' potential so that they can acquire systematized forms of knowledge that do not constitute a privilege for elites only.

The curriculum is a crucial component of the school operation. Perspectives on its design are directly connected with educational and social policies and strategic planning, and they clash on both the level of theory and that of practice.

As we shall see, Freire's position that educational content should be based on the learners' thematic universe comes into direct conflict with the traditional perspective on curriculum planning, the content of which is founded on the traditions of the previous generations, represents what is perceived as the highest expression of Western civilization, and is organized into separate subjects. Freire also breaks with the dominant perspective of social efficiency on curriculum planning, which aims to supply, via behavioral objectives, the knowledge and skills deemed necessary for the efficient functioning of the economy and the society, treats learners as passive receivers of knowledge, and assigns to curriculum a technical character disarticulated from social, political, or ideological conflicts. In addition, Freire's ideas on curriculum planning differ radically from the multiform versions of a child-centered perspective. The Brazilian educator does not focus on studying the child in an abstract or ahistorical framework, nor does he adopt an individualistic interpretation that fetishizes spontaneity. His position, whereby the themes connecting learners with the world become an object of systematic research and comprise the foundations of the curriculum content, is the basic precondition to ensure learners' active participation in the educational process. However, establishing the curriculum on a meticulous investigation of learners' thematic universe does not lead to the fetishization of student or popular knowledge. Neither does this type of curriculum planning undervalue the importance of systematized forms of knowledge.

In contrast to the other perspectives that have traditionally dominated the curriculum field, Freire's perspective provides a fertile ground for those teachers and anybody involved in the struggle for the formation of a new sociopolitical majority, which can open the way for a radical transformation of contemporary societies with a socialist orientation. This transformation is increasingly becoming imperative for a number of serious reasons, such as the use of unending wars as an indispensable component of imperialist domination; the rise of class and racial inequalities; the curtailing of democratic freedoms and social rights; the increasing totalitarian character of contemporary nations and the strengthening of mechanisms of oppression and control; the prevailing culture of individualism, fear, and passivity; the tight control of the mass media by big business; and the large-scale ecological destruction that is threatening our planet. The dilemma "Socialism or Barbarism" put forward by Rosa Luxemburg at the beginning of the twentieth century appears to still be relevant today. Freire's pedagogy, which is in direct opposition to both the pedagogies of bourgeois dominance and the pedagogies of the bureaucratization of the first socialist countries, can be instrumental in ensuring that the second half of this dilemma—barbarism—does not prevail.

I

THE FORMATION OF A RADICAL LIBERAL EDUCATOR

⤚⟩

FIRST STEPS

Paulo Reglus Neves Freire became well known in Brazil and around the world as Paulo Freire. He was born on September 19, 1921, in Recife, in northeast Brazil.

At the end of the nineteenth century, Recife was rapidly developing, mainly as a result of the establishment of sugar refineries. As commerce and public services expanded, the city attracted the poor as well as the middle classes like a magnet. In 1920, its population was 239,000 and growing, bringing about the expansion of state and federal public services and of police and military establishments. Paulo's father, an officer of the military police, was born in Rio Grande do Norte. He married Edeltrudes Neves from Pernambuco. When Paulo, the youngest of four children, was born, his family lived in a city divided into two different sections: one for the members of the upper and middle classes, who lived in spacious houses, and the other for the poor, who were almost half of Recife's population and lived in barracks. By 1923, the infant mortality rate in Recife was higher than that in any other Brazilian city. A spiritualist father who

Chapter 1

cared for his family and a devoted Catholic mother gave Freire, as he himself used to say, the best years of his life. Freedom of choice, tolerance, and dialogue were the characteristics of his first learning environment. As Freire would recount later, "My father's respect for my mother's religious belief taught me from infancy to respect the choices of others" (Jeria 1986: 6).

According to Ireland, during the 1920s and 1930s the expansion of industry in southeast Brazil was based on political and economic stagnation in the northeast. An alliance between landowners and bourgeoisie had to be maintained and supported, so that Brazil's bourgeois hegemony would not be threatened. This entailed safeguarding the sanctity of pre-established forms of landownership. Furthermore, manufacturers in south Brazil were not interested in the industrialization of the northeast because they wanted to secure a domestic "colonial" market for their products and to avoid possible competition from that region (Ireland 1987: 12–13). The economic crisis in the United States and Europe at the end of the 1920s caused great blows to Brazilian economic and political life. Coffee and sugar barons who took advantage of the colonization system were thrown out by the federal government thanks to Getúlio Vargas's liberal revolution. Landowners, the bourgeoisie, and the petit bourgeoisie formed a liberal coalition and took control of political matters. For the first time in Brazilian history, the masses began to take part in political life, and the army was supportive of the whole endeavor (Morray 1968: 103–104).

The 1930s proved to be quite difficult for the Freire family. Paulo's father lost his job as a military officer due to the economic depression that had begun in 1929. The family could no longer maintain the same living standards and moved to Jabotão, a city fifteen miles west of Recife. The loss of the house in Recife exemplified the loss of prestige for the family. His father subsequently died in 1934, and according to Freire, from that period on his family would try to keep a petit-bourgeoisie identity through "status objects," such as a German piano, that would link them to a social status they could no longer enjoy. In Jabotão, Freire had to face many problems. Young

12

Paulo had to become very resourceful in order to overcome his hunger: he killed birds with a sling, went fishing, and even had to steal. However, it was in Jabotão that he "dealt intimately with rural and urban kids, the sons and daughters of rural and urban workers" (Jeria 1986: 9–10; Freire 1996a: 81; Araujo 2001: 38). Freire recounts this experience by emphasizing that it helped him "to get used to a different way of thinking and expressing" himself. As he says, "This was the grammar of the people, the language of the people, and as an educator of the people I devote myself today to the rigorous understanding of this language" (Gadotti 1994: 3).

According to Jeria, during his early school years Freire fell behind his schoolmates, and some of his teachers believed that he was mildly mentally retarded. In his own words: "The times I spent repeating France's capital Paris, England's capital London … But the only geography I could understand at that time was the geography of my hunger and not London and Paris. It did not make sense. So it was tremendously difficult and at that time I thought I was stupid because I was not able to understand what I was reading." In 1937, at the age of sixteen, Paulo Freire entered secondary school with many difficulties. At that time, Brazilian education consisted of three levels: primary (four years), middle (first cycle, or *gimnasio*, four years, and second cycle, or *collegio*, three or four years), and higher. Middle-level school consisted of three branches, "secondary," "technical," and "normal," with the latter preparing students to become primary school teachers. Although all three branches were supposed to be equivalent, the academic branch (secondary) was actually considered the most prestigious and attracted more than 80 percent of all middle-school students (Jeria 1986: 10–11).

As Owensby notes, during the 1930s and 1940s Brazilian secondary schools were the training ground for white-collar employees and expanded between 250 and 300 percent (Owensby 1999: 88). Macedo informs us that Freire had difficulty entering a secondary school because his family could not afford the tuition. His mother had to appeal to the generosity of several school owners before Aluisio Araujo, owner of the Oswaldo

Cruz School, gave him the opportunity to attend free of charge (Macedo 2001: 6). Araujo played an important role in Freire's education by directing his interest to Christian humanism and by developing his democratic spirit (McLaren 2000: 142).

When Paulo completed his secondary studies, he was qualified to teach Portuguese and got a position at the University of Recife. In 1943, he married Elza Maria Costa de Oliveira from Recife, an elementary school teacher. According to Freire, Elza exercised a strong influence on his work; she encouraged him and collaborated with him on several projects and influenced him while he was writing his books, especially *Pedagogy of the Oppressed*. His forty years with Elza were, according to Freire, "an extension of the dialogue that I learned with my parents" (Jeria 1986: 13).

During his studies, at the age of twenty-one, and after refraining from practicing Catholicism for almost a year, Freire joined the youth of the Catholic Action group, which aimed to disseminate generally accepted Catholic ideas and to stimulate religiously approved behavior at the university by means of the active participation of Catholic militants. In Brazil this group seemed more concerned with spiritual matters than social reality. However, the university group in Recife that Freire joined was more sensitive to the conditions of poverty and hunger in northeast Brazil and approached social change as a solution to these social problems.

By the 1940s, the Dom Vital Center (Centro Dom Vital) had risen to prominence under the direction of the Brazilian Christian philosopher Tristão de Atayde, who, after moving away from his earlier positions, was influenced by the teachings of Jacques Maritain and thus supported a more social view of the church and religion. The center organized a series of seminars for discussion of the works of the French philosophers Maritain and Emanuel Mounier. It also expanded its activity to other cities, Recife being one of them. Many of those who took part in these seminars played an important role in forming a more progressive stance in the Brazilian church during the late 1960s and early 1970s. Among them, Hélder Cámara, who later became archbishop, was one of Freire's best friends and supporters of his work. The Dom Vital Center played an important role in creating the University Catholic Action group, the Catholic Institute of Higher Studies (later Catholic University of Rio de Janeiro), and the National Confederation of Catholic Workers.

Even though the Dom Vital Center discussed and disseminated the ideas of the French Christian philosophers who favored social change, pluralism, and democracy, young Paulo did not confine himself only to the study of such texts. He became interested in reading classical Portuguese and Brazilian authors (such as Carneiro Ribeiro and Ruy Barbosa) and, through these readings, became interested in grammar, syntax, and the philosophy and psychology of language.

In parallel with his readings, Freire taught Portuguese at the *gimnasio* from which he had graduated, an instruction he later considered to be quite naïve. His work as a teacher gave him the opportunity to help his family financially. At the age of twenty-five, after having abandoned the idea of practicing law and having committed himself to studying Portuguese and European philosophers, Freire decided to accept an offer to become director of the Department of Education and Culture at the newly formed Social Service of Industry (SESI) in Pernambuco (Jeria 1986: 12–21).

In 1942, Vargas, the dictator and leader of the so-called New State of Brazil (Brazil's Estado Novo), created the National Service for Industrial Training, which according to Evans was one of the first vocational training centers in Latin America (Evans 1986: 40). Vargas's policy and ideology had already established him as a paradigmatic example of a populist leader. As French mentions, populism was a nationalist and multiclass movement, typically urban in nature, that was characterized by an eclectic ideology, a clientelistic relation to the masses, and the existence of a charismatic leader (another typical example of a populist leader was Juan Perón in Argentina). Populism emerged in Latin America during a crisis of oligarchic parliamentarianism and a search for alternatives to export-oriented economic strategies. Its essential characteristic was the transformation and control of the labor movement by a linking of the trade unions directly to the state. Within the Latin American context, Brazilian state intervention in industrial and labor relations was a paradigmatic example of corporatism in which the state played a major role in structuring, supporting, and regulating interest groups and aimed at controlling their internal affairs as well as the relationships between them (French 1992: 4).

As Weinstein mentions, Eurico Dutra, Vargas's successor, created the SESI four years later. In São Paulo, the activities of the new agency were meant to confront the labor movement. Among the agency's most important activities were providing food for industrial workers at work sites; creating medical clinics in working-class neighborhoods; teaching Brazilian workers the rudiments of good nutrition; fighting illiteracy; organizing visits at work sites, sports facilities, churches, schools, and labor unions; and offering counseling for all kinds of issues (ranging from legal assistance to recommendations against participating in strikes). SESI served as a vehicle in the Dutra government's anticommunist crusade. It also contributed to securing social peace by creating a climate of collaboration between employers and employees for the expansion of national production and social welfare (Weinstein 1996: 1, 18, 114–115, 140, 146–151).

Galenson and Araujo seem to confirm these analyses of SESI's fundamental characteristics, which Freire never denied (Galenson 1962: 178; Araujo 1999: 211–212; Freire 1996a: 82). In fact, Freire said SESI was set up "to confuse reality and to put obstacles in the way of the working class achieving its own identity" (Gadotti 1994: 6). However, according to autobiographical references included in his book *Letters to Cristina,* his work during the ten years he spent in Pernambuco was very different from the work that was done in other regions (Freire 1996a). Alexander attests to the truth of this when he notes that, thanks to the agency's decentralized nature, there were three quite different tendencies reflected in its administration. SESI's administration in São Paulo gave priority to developing charitable operations; in the region of Rio de Janeiro, it contributed to the political advancement of the industrialist class; in the states of Pernambuco and Rio Grande do Sul, SESI's administration favored helping individuals, groups, and the community at large, so that its members could, in turn, help themselves (Alexander 1962: 106–111).

One of the action plans in Pernambuco that Freire participated in was the democratization of the relationship among the educators, the learners, their parents, the school, and the community. This democratization was achieved through the educators' understanding of various types of teaching aimed at transcending the mechanical transfer of knowledge and at establishing a critical way of teaching. Nonetheless, even though the goal was right, the method for its achievement was wrong: "We contradicted ourselves, first, by not listening to the people with whom we were working concerning what they would like to discuss and, second, by choosing ourselves the lecture themes" (Freire 1996a: 90–91).

During the years of Freire's pedagogical experimentations in SESI, possibilities for a different political future in Brazil started to emerge. In 1951, Vargas regained power. According to Jaguaribe, during Dutra's government Vargas had been a senator and he succeeded in becoming a reliable "dictator mutated into a politician" by organizing the Brazilian Workers Party (or PTB). His party soon turned into one of the most important movements in Brazil because it combined massive participation and the "philosophy of 'laborism'" (which had always been one of Vargas's most attractive ideas). Social welfare combined with anticapitalist rhetoric and economic nationalism became very popular and led him to a victorious election in 1950. Vargas's controversial ideology had three distinguishing characteristics: his politically innovative views during the 1920s and early 1930s, his quasi-fascist policy in the late 1930s, and his fervent support of a welfare state after World War II up until his suicide. All three corresponded with the differing expectations and the various roles of the middle class as it emerged from the margins of Brazilian political life and headed toward full participation in the political scene of that era (Jaguaribe 1972: 48–49).

After his reelection, Vargas continued to attack foreign companies and their big profits in Brazil. These speeches were very popular in Brazil at that time and of great importance to political developments during the next decade. It is worth noting at this point the expansion of his influence on the left. Joao Goulart, a young leftist, became a member of the cabinet and assumed office as labor minister in 1953. Soon he became the black sheep for the middle class and the military hierarchy because he was considered a demagogue. One year later, taking advantage of his lawful right to give a pay raise to employees, he increased all salaries by 100 percent, and the very same day he was dismissed from office by Vargas (Bruneau 1974: 59).

As we shall see, Goulart played an important role in the dramatic political developments of the next decade. However, according to Barnard, the president's position became quite difficult due to galloping inflation, as well as the absence of changes in the Brazilian economic infrastructure. A daunting drought in the northeastern part of the country aggravated the situation even further. Eventually, after facing formidable opposition from the military in carrying through his policies and a mood of growing political hysteria, with the media making accusations of scandals, Vargas ended up committing suicide (Barnard 1980: 26–27).

RADICALIZATION

According to Araujo and Macedo, although Freire resigned from the post of superintendent at the Department of Education and Culture at SESI in Pernambuco in October 1956, the director of SESI-National requested that he be seconded to the Division of Research and Planning in 1957. Thus, Freire traveled as a consultant from October 1957 until April 14, 1961, through several Brazilian states. At the end of 1959, after earning his doctorate, he was tenured as professor of history and philosophy of education at the School of Philosophy, Science, and Arts, at the University of Recife. The title of his doctoral thesis was "Education in Modern Brazil" and "Education as the Practice of Freedom" was based on it. "Education as the Practice of Freedom" is one of his most popular and most important essays, and it marked his first period of thought and action (Araujo and Macedo 1998: 15–16).

Freire started his academic career in the same year that Miguel Arraes got elected as Recife's mayor and went on to implement a number of social plans, including the creation of the Movement for Popular Culture (MCP). Freire, in his capacity as coordinator for the program of adult education, collaborated quite closely with MCP. Arraes was a candidate for governor supported by the Popular Front of Recife, which was created in 1946 and included communists, socialists, leftist Catholics, and the left wing of both the Brazilian Workers Party and the Social Democratic Party (Facundo 1984: 3). It is important to understand the creation of MCP in light of the more general radicalization of the Brazilian popular social classes at the end of the 1950s and the beginning of the 1960s.

New president Juscelino Kubitschek de Oliveira's administration in 1956 attempted to launch rapid industrialization based on his plan of "fifty years of progress in five." At the same time, according to Hall and Garcia, Kubitschek favored the democratization of political life, which, in turn, made possible a reorganization of the labor movement, whose leaders preferred to organize their unions (most of which were illegal) and federations into pacts, alliances, and so forth, instead of attacking governmental corporatist control. This kind of reorganization led to a coalition of laborists, communists, Catholics, and independents that gained control of the National Confederation of Industrial Workers, previously dominated by government-controlled unionists. These developments had important political effects on the labor movement in the early 1960s (Hall and Garcia 1989: 179–180).

The creation of the Peasant Leagues (LC) was another very important factor in the radicalization of the lower social classes. The creation of LC in 1955 started as a reaction against the eviction of peasants who had been renting land on a sugar farm since the 1930s. The peasants then decided to organize themselves into a mutual aid community and asked a local lawyer, Francisco Julião,[1] for help. The peasant leagues grew rapidly not

19

only as cooperative groups, but also as an organized political force in which Julião played an important role. Since most members of the leagues were illiterate, and, according to the legislature, they were unable to take part in the official political processes,[2] there was increasing pressure to take measures to fight illiteracy (Jeria 1986: 26–27).

The peasant leagues were based on a growing class consciousness, and conservative social and political groups considered them a serious threat. The Catholic Church, as Bruneau contends, viewed with distrust the emerging popular leaders of this period (Bruneau 1974: 66). Although Julião was a socialist, he posed a threat as great as any communist, and his influence during the 1960s was immense. Lionel Brizola, Goulart's brother-in-law, a leftist demagogue, opposed the church in Rio Grande do Sul. The danger from the Left was becoming much more imminent, particularly after the victory of the revolution in Cuba in 1959, and the lesson for the rural areas was quite obvious.

According to related reports, the peasant leagues in Pernambuco had a peasant-proletarian character. The most active among them were located in the sugar zone where wage laborers predominated, rather than in the regions where peasant smallholders constituted the majority of the population. This is why, in the early 1960s, the number of unions oriented mainly to wage laborers outstripped the peasant leagues. In less than twelve months, almost thirteen hundred rural labor unions were registered. The successful organization of two strikes in Pernambuco in 1963 (84,000 laborers participated in the first strike; 230,000 participated in the second one), after which wages rose by 80 percent, was experienced by many workers as a decisive moment toward their liberation and the recognition of their citizenship. In the same year, Pernambuco union leaders participated in the foundation of the National Confederation of Rural Workers (Pereira 1997: 97; Elias 1973: 68).

Furthermore, it is important to consider at this point developments in the Brazilian Catholic Church. The Catholic Action Youth broke up, and many former members joined another organization, Popular Action (AP), which was politically more active and did not follow guidelines from the church hierarchy. Although its ideology was far from Marxism-Leninism, its members believed in the necessity of fighting capitalism, which they considered alienating and exploitative (Ireland 1987: 22). AP was a movement of "intellectuals for the people" that shared the disappointment that neo-Marxists and humanitarian socialists felt in the results of the Russian Revolution, and that also accused the Brazilian communists of a lack of true revolutionary perspective (Coben 1998: 61).

Popular Action started operating in 1961 and was officially launched in June 1962, rapidly gaining supporters from the middle class and the radical intellectuals. Its positions were based on the writings of Teilhard de Chardin, Emanuel Mounier, and Pope John XXIII. AP claimed that the development of history was not a simple evolutionary process but a dialectic one in which human struggle played an important role. This dialectic struggle would give rise to historical consciousness, which would be a critical, conscious reflection on the historical process. This consciousness would arise only when the individual examined the world in a critical manner so that she or he could act upon it and transform it. This process was called "humanization." The end product of the historical struggle would be the creation of utopia, a concept similar to Christ's Kingdom of Heaven or Karl Marx's classless society (Jarvis 1987: 265–267). Many of the members of this movement, who were organizing labor unions and peasant leagues and who also participated in what were called "culture circles," were about to play an important role in the dissemination of Freire's ideas on literacy.

The formation of the Movement for the Education of the Base (MEB) was another sign of the radicalization taking place in the Brazilian Catholic Church. MEB originally started as radio schools in the bishoprics of Natal and Arakagio; their aim was to propagate educational programs as well as programs on health and nurture. A basic characteristic of this movement was its democratic operation. All those who participated in the movement, from directors to simple members, considered the operation of MEB an element of democratizing social structures.

The most important among MEB's objectives was to stop under-development by helping to create structural reforms that would make communities self-sufficient. MEB aimed to bring about structural reform by making the masses literate, organizing them into workers associations, and training their community leaders, who would acquire political power and challenge the existing structures (Van Vugt 1991: 103–104).

As Facundo stresses, the central goal of the Brazilian progressive forces during those years was not revolution in the sense of armed struggle for structural transformation. The goal was democratic reform and capitalist national development. The political program for the attainment of the goal was mostly formulated by the Social Institute of Brazilian Studies (ISEB), which was very active during the 1950s and early 1960s (Facundo 1984: 2).

Among the most important writers who influenced ISEB's Brazilian intellectuals was Karl Mannheim (Torres 1993: 140). According to Frank, ISEB was one of the institutions founded in Latin American countries by national elements of the bourgeois class who believed that, had Latin American countries developed their domestic economy, their commerce would not have fallen into decline, nor would there have been any problems with their industrialization. In this view, Latin American countries should follow their own course toward national capitalist development (Frank 1972: 150–151).

Freire repeatedly used the writings of ISEB intellectuals and commented positively on ISEB's work because it approached Brazil as a subject, not as an object. Turning their back on their own world, the majority of Brazilian intellectuals suffered because Brazil was not Europe or the United States. ISEB's intellectuals placed themselves at the service of the national culture. It was not by accident that ISEB, although itself not a university, spoke to an entire generation of university professors and although not a workers' organization, organized conferences along with trade unions (Freire 1974: 39–40).

In the fall of 1960, the election of Janio Quadros as president of the country brought new hope for change. Brazil was entering a time that would be a period of crisis for some and a period of revolution for others. Some would call it a time of transition; others, a period of confusion. However, all agreed that society was moving toward new forms of power relationships, with the emergence of a new society on the horizon. During Quadros's short term (he resigned a year after being elected), his government launched an anti-inflationary program and opened diplomatic relations with the Soviet Union. Quadros's resignation brought confusion to conservative Brazilians because the new president, Goulart, who was also PTB's president, symbolized the communist menace (Jeria 1986: 33).

In this social and political reality, the first version of what became known as the "Paulo Freire method" was formed within the framework of MCP in the municipality of Recife. This very radicalization of the popular social classes, which included MCP, was one of the most important features of Freire's literacy program.

According to Freire, MCP's primary aim was the creation of a service, pedagogical in nature, that would work *with* the lower social classes and not *above* them, work *with* them and not *for* them. The men and women who would be involved with the movement would be partners in the same adventure and not just technicians or specialists. The only precondition for those who would join the movement was to have a common dream: to transform Brazilian society and to fight for it. Another equally important MCP aim was the critical understanding of the role of culture in the educational process, as well as in the political struggle for social change. Also among MCP's aims was the preservation of traditions: the people's festivals, their stories, their legends, and their religiousness, all of which were characterized not only by forms of resignation but also by forms of resistance.

MCP operated as a movement, not as an institution of popular education, by focusing on the development of projects rather than on the creation of departments, which indicated the movement's nonbureaucratic spirit. This style of MCP's operation never became random or permissive. The cultural circles were spaces where teaching and learning took place in dialogic form; where learning, not knowledge transfer, occurred; where knowledge was produced, not simply presented or imposed on the learners; where new hypotheses for reading the world were created. The cultural circles functioned as cultural centers that included libraries, theatrical presentations, and recreational and sports activities.

The educators working in the cultural circles were young university students who joined the movement as volunteers, and it was up to them to decide how they wanted to contribute. After a brief preparation, they would begin working under the supervision of the team coordinating the project at hand. Cultural circles could be formed almost anywhere (philanthropic organizations, soccer clubs, neighborhood associations, churches). The educators were in charge of preparing these circles after organizing visits and talks at the corresponding sites. Once two or three circles had been formed, the educators would conduct a thematic assessment among the participants. The team coordinating the project would analyze the assessment, develop the themes, and organize a program to be discussed with the participants of the circle. The number of meetings varied from circle to circle because of the different interests and potential of the circle members.

After a few thematic assessments, the fundamental topics revealed by the research were developed: nationalism, democracy, development, imperialism, the vote for illiterates, rural reform, profit remittances abroad, illiteracy, and exclusion from education. These were some of the topics that people from the lower social classes in Recife were interested in during the 1960s. The results were impressive. The interest that this work generated, the liveliness of the discussions, and the critical curiosity and learning ability that the groups demonstrated made Freire and his colleagues think about developing a similar procedure focusing on adult literacy. However, the whole project became the target of attacks by several MCP members. Attacks also came from the Left. These attacks were directed against the point of view of the role of culture in the educational process and especially the role of popular culture—a point of view that they considered to be "idealistically bourgeois" (Freire 1996a: 110–111, 116–117, 120–122).

Freire's first encounter with adult education was through MCP. The cultural circles offered a new approach to learning and, as he mentions in "Education as the Practice of Freedom," "instead of a teacher, we had a coordinator; instead of lectures, dialogue; instead of pupils, group participants; instead of alienating syllabi, compact programs that were 'broken down' and codified into learning units" (Freire 1974: 42). To use Freire's words, the cultural circles

> had no program a priori. The program came about as the result of consultation with the groups; in other words, the themes would be discussed in the cultural circles; the group would decide. We, as educators, should develop the theme that was to be discussed. However, we could add themes, which, in *Pedagogy of the Oppressed*, I called "hinge themes"—subjects that would be inserted as fundamental elements in the entire corpus and that would clarify the theme proposed by the people's group.... The positive results that I obtained from this were so considerable on a number of levels—political involvement, understanding, critical reading—that I thought: If it is possible to do this, to reach this level of discussion with popular groups, regardless of their being literate or not, why couldn't it be done within a literacy scheme? Why couldn't the students of a literacy scheme become politically involved in the setting up of their system of graphic signs as subjects rather than objects of this system? (cited in Gadotti 1994: 17–18)

In October 1962, the mayor of Recife, who had taken the initiative to found MCP and had assigned the coordination of the adult education project to Freire, decided to run for governor in Pernambuco. Arraes won the elections due to two major advantages: his successes as a mayor and the prestige of his close relationships with President Quadros and his successor, Goulart. Arraes's election was a clear indication that Brazil was moving toward a more complex political situation than had ever before been seen.

In light of this new reality, the Department of Cultural Extension Service (SEC) was created at the University of Recife. SEC aimed at diffusing culture and popular education. The university, according to the official document outlining the rationale behind the new operation, had to overcome its traditional role and participate dynamically in the process of social change. It was considered essential that in northeastern Brazil the conditions be created for a progressive dissemination of culture and for the integration of the university in the regional reality. The objectives of this extension were to be achieved through the organization of conferences, publications, and radio programs. Considered to be of equal importance for the attainment of these objectives was the initiation of contacts with workers' and peasants' unions, as well as with all intellectuals, whether affiliated with a university or not. Professor Paulo Freire was named director of SEC.

Freire was now in a position where he could try implementing his method for adult education on a large scale. On December 3, 1962, President Goulart agreed that Aluisio Alves (governor of Rio Grante do Norte) could sign an "elementary education agreement" with the United States Agency for International Development (USAID). The agreement reflected the opinion of a number of people at the USAID station who did not want to implement educational programs in the area of Pernambuco, where they felt they would face problems arising from the political power of the Left. However, there were others who supported implementing a program in Recife in order to counteract the Left's increasing influence.

President Goulart's approval of the project was expected because emphasis on education was one of the most important issues in his government's platform. This agreement offered him a good opportunity to underline his government's interest in building schools and teacher-training centers (including a teacher-training institute) and creating audiovisual center supplies and services. Freire, through the auspices of the university, participated in the city of Angicos' project in Rio Grande do Norte. The impact his method had in Recife was enough for the state government of Rio Grande do Norte and USAID to consent to the use of the "Freire method" in a short-term project (Jeria 1986: 34–37).

Facundo notes that Freire's acceptance of USAID created tensions among the forces of the Left; the implementation of the program was seen by some leftists as a threat to the Popular Front's planned electoral strategy in Rio Grante do Norte. Tensions were minimized when Freire secured two important concessions: (1) there would be no interference from authorities with the content of his program, and (2) participants would be incorporated at all program levels, including program direction (Facundo 1984: 4).

In the Angicos project, more than 70 teachers were trained to teach 299 illiterate land laborers for forty-five days. President Goulart attended the final hour of some classes, thereby giving national recognition to Freire's efforts. The positive results of the Angicos project made Freire's work quite popular not only in the northeast but also among people all over Brazil. Nevertheless, there were many who opposed his work. Although USAID director James Howe declared that "contrary to the allegations (such as those in the newspaper *O Globo*) the method of Paulo Freire is really a method of Marxist indoctrination, the technicians (people who are technically familiar with writing programs) have affirmed that this method on its own and in the specific case of Angicos does not have a political or social orientation" (Jeria 1986: 38). However, either due to pressures or to organizational problems, USAID support for the literacy project was discontinued in January 1964.

By 1963, there were at least three campaigns for the fight against illiteracy in Brazil: (1) the SEC's experimental work, led by Freire, at the university of Recife, in the northeastern part of the country; (2) the work of a group of young Catholic students, led by the National Conference of Bishops of Brazil (which was funded by the government through MEB), who used Freire's approach to literacy; and (3) the work of MCP, which spread throughout Brazil and was organized on the basis of discussion groups without having literacy as its primary objective.

The idea of implementing a national literacy program was more easily accepted after Paulo De Tarso's appointment as minister of education. Although he was a member of the Christian Democratic Party, he was considered a radical. De Tarso, a former member of Catholic Action, was a personal friend of Freire's and was acquainted with the work done in Recife. Educational reform had to include a national literacy program, and because Freire's ideas were very popular all over Brazil, De Tarso had no difficulty in selecting Freire as the program's director.

The idea of establishing a massive literacy program had a tremendous political and social impact on Brazil in 1963, if we take into consideration that it provided millions of people with the right to participate in the political affairs of their country, a right they had been deprived of because they were illiterate. The project, like the one in Angicos, provided people with the means to learn to read and write in forty hours. There was an abundance of coordinators for the project, but training them was a real problem (Jeria 1986: 37–41).

In the meantime, according to Barnard, in 1963, by means of a referendum, Goulart managed to regain the power that Congress had deprived him of at the beginning of his term. At the same time, he started traveling up and down the Brazilian countryside to promote agrarian reform. Furthermore, he assisted in organizing the unions and the National Confederation of Peasant Laborers with the aim of uniting all peasants. The period of reconciliation had come to an end: reform and opposition to imperialism were now part of the promotion of the "state of the poor." The middle and bourgeois classes were threatened by Goulart's attitude. The government administration of the Brazilian states, the army, the mass media, and the state services were all hostile. Optimism, however, continued to expand throughout the Left.[3] Almost everybody was convinced that the time for democratization had come.

Goulart promised tax reform, the nationalization of foreign property, and the monitoring of property rental rates. He organized a series of massive rallies; his opponents retaliated with counterdemonstrations. The arrest of forty marines who attempted to unionize the navy resulted in sedition by one hundred marines. Goulart did not allow their punishment, and the admiral who was held responsible resigned. This incident propelled forward the military coup that was already in the works. On April 1, 1964, the military came to power and the Brazilian president was exiled to Uruguay (Barnard 1980: 29–31)

THE LITERACY PROGRAM

Freire was arrested and exiled to Bolivia, but after a short time he was forced to leave for health reasons and ended up in Chile, where, in 1968–1969, he wrote a book that was to gain world-wide attention. This book was *Pedagogy of the Oppressed*. A year earlier, he had already published an essay in Portuguese entitled "Education as the Practice of Freedom," which was based on the dissertation he had submitted to the University of Recife in 1959. It was the first part of a volume published in English under the title *Education: The Practice of Freedom*. The essay had been written in 1965 (Goulet 1974: vii). This text is characteristic of the first phase of the development of his thought and action, which allows us to understand his political positions, as well as his positions about planning a literacy program.

In this essay, Freire's political positions were grounded both ontologically and historically. Their ontological basis was characterized by essentialist logic, according to which human beings differ from animals because they engage in relationships with others and with the world. They experience that world as an objective and independent reality, a reality that they are capable of getting to know. Animals, submerged within reality, cannot relate to it; they can merely come into contact with it. The ability of human beings to separate from and be open to the world distinguishes them as relational beings. Human relationships with the world are multifaceted in nature.

When faced with different challenges or even with the same challenge, human beings organize themselves, choose the best response, control themselves, act, and change through their re-actions without being limited to a single reaction pattern. They do all this consciously, as if they were using a tool to deal with a problem. They relate to their world in a critical way. They perceive the objective data of their reality (and the way these data relate to each other) through reflection and not by reflex as animals do. It is through this act of critical perception that human beings discover their own temporality by reaching back to yesterday, recognizing today, and coming upon tomorrow.

Freire emphasizes particular sets of contrasts: the *active* versus the *passive* role of human beings, *integration* as distinguished from *adaptation,* and person as *subject* as against person as *object.* The first element in each of these contrasts constitutes the basis of humanization. In other words, these characteristics make human beings capable of creating history and culture. The second element, each of which is symptomatic of dehumanization, makes humans lose their basic ontological characteristics. The processes of humanization and dehumanization, although in competition with each other, coexist.

Brazil entered a transitory phase toward the end of the nineteenth century as a result of restrictions on the slave trade in 1850 and the abolition of slavery in 1888. The capital intended for the purchase of slaves was invested in industrial activity instead. Brazilian industrialization received a strong emphasis in the 1920s, as well as in the period following World War II when the urban areas of the country were rapidly developing. These changes influenced Brazil's national life. More specifically, there appeared new tendencies in culture, the arts, literature, and science toward self-identification in terms of the Brazilian reality. This identification included a focus on planning solutions rather than importing them: "The country had begun to find itself. The people emerged and began to participate in the historical process" (Freire 1974: 21–31).

According to Freire, this transitory phase became an arena of conflict as people and institutions began to divide into two general, opposing groups: reactionaries and progressives. The deepening of the clash between old and new encouraged radicalization, which involved increased commitment to the choices a person made. Radicalization, Freire proposes, is predominantly critical, communicative, loving, and humble. The person who has made a radical choice should not deny another person's right to choose or try to impose that radical choice on others. The rights of the other should be respected; it is acceptable to make an effort to convert but not to crush an opponent. However, the radical has the duty, imposed by love itself, to react against the violence of those who try to silence him or her and those who, in the name of freedom, kill freedom. To be radical does not involve self-flagellation. Radicals cannot passively accept a situation in which the excessive power of a few leads to the dehumanization of all (Freire 1974: 10–11).

In Freire's view, radical positions were adopted principally, but not exclusively, by groups of Christians who believed, along with Mounier, that (a) both the history of the world and the history of human beings had meaning; (b) progress is constant, despite diverse vicissitudes that may complicate its route; (c) the development of science and technique that characterized the modern Western era and its spread worldwide constituted a decisive aspect of liberation; and (d) progressive people were charged with the task of liberating themselves.

As for the period before the coup in 1964, Freire explained that, although he was not in favor of rebellion, he considered it one of the most promising aspects of political life because it represented a sign of advancement, an "introduction to a more complete humanity." He was convinced that Brazilian people could not acquire social and political responsibility unless they experienced it through intervention in the destiny of their children's schools; their trade unions, clubs, councils; and every form of social institution. Democracy, according to Freire, should depend on the achievement of economic development, which would be autonomous and national in character but would not limit itself to technical questions, pure economic policy, or structural reform. Democracy should involve the passage from one mentality to another because it primarily constitutes a way of life, not merely a form of governing. Educators would contribute to the birth of a new society by espousing a critical education. Democracy and democratic education ought to be founded on faith in the people, on the belief that they not only should but also can discuss the problems of their country, their continent, their world, their work, and democracy itself. Education as an act of love and courage cannot fear the analysis of reality or avoid creative discussion (Freire 1974: 29, 32, 35–36, 38).

Freire was in favor of an education that would contribute to finding solutions for the problems the Brazilian people faced. However, these solutions were not supposed to be imposed upon the people or discovered *for* them; they were to be discovered *with* the people. He proposed an education that would enable people to reflect upon themselves, their responsibilities, and their role in the new cultural climate, but mostly reflect on or realize their own power of reflection. Such an education would help people to adopt an inquisitive attitude toward their problems, thus contributing to the establishment and operation of an authentic democracy.

Nonetheless, there were those who subverted democracy by presenting it in a number of ways: by making it appear irrational, rigid, and hateful; by poisoning it with fear; by making it an instrument of the powerful in the oppression of the weak; by militarizing it against the people; by alienating a nation in its name. Contrary to all the aforementioned, democracy does not provoke fear in people. It eliminates privileges, it can plan without becoming rigid, and it can defend itself as it is nourished by a critical spirit. In short, Freire defended a "militant democracy" and a corresponding education (Freire 1974: 16, 36, 58).[4]

According to the Brazilian educator, traditional curricula could never develop a critical consciousness because they were disconnected from life, focused on words emptied of the reality they represented, and lacking in concrete activity (Freire 1974: 37). Freire strongly believed that the formation of a critical consciousness should be the central and most important educational goal included in a curriculum. This educational goal was connected with the realization of a militant democracy, which he considered to be its central political goal—a goal essential to Brazil's process of self-reliant socioeconomic development. The development of critical consciousness would represent what Freire called *"conscientização"* (conscientization).

According to Freire, the term *conscientization* became popular thanks to a friend of his, Hélder Cámara, bishop of Recife (Schipani 1984: 151). O'Gorman notes that the term originally came from ISEB groups, and it became popularized in other countries thanks to Cámara (O'Gorman 1978: 53). According to another report inside the Catholic Church in Brazil, *conscientização* was approached in two different ways: either as part of a revolutionary program in which the masses and the oppressed could espouse social transformation, or as a way to integrate marginalized groups into the most modern sectors of Brazilian society so that they, too, could take part in the national development of Brazil and share the advantages of this process (Streck 1977: 97–98).

Freire describes conscientization as a process consisting of three stages. The first, *semi-intransitivity*, is characterized by people's inability to perceive problems that lie outside the orbit of biological necessities, as well as the inability to experience life located in a historical context. As people enhance their power to apprehend problems and respond to suggestions and questions arising in their context, they enter into dialogue not only with other people but also with the world, thus entering into the second stage, that of *transitive consciousness.* By extending their interests and concerns beyond their biological necessities, people become "transitive" and are almost totally engaged with existence. However, there is also an initial stage of transitive consciousness, that of *naïve transitivity.*

The achievement of *critical transitive consciousness*—the third stage in the conscientization process—implies the capacity to interpret problems in depth, the substitution of causal principles for magical explanations, the testing of one's discoveries, the positive disposition to revise, the attempt to avoid distortion in the perception of problems, the rejection of passive positions, the practice of dialogue rather than polemics, receptivity to the new for reasons beyond mere novelty, restraining of the impulse to reject the old merely because it is old, acceptance of what is valid in both old and new (Freire 1974: 18–19).

Although Freire considered that people could advance to naïve transitivity as a result of infrastructure transformations, he believed that the passage from naïve transitivity to critical transitivity came only through serious educational efforts aimed at that goal. Later he acknowledged that he had not avoided idealistic subjectivism in his discussions on the relations between awareness and the world. As for the process of consciousness-raising, he admitted making the mistake of not having addressed the dialectical relationship between knowledge of reality and transformation of reality, implying that the unveiling of reality automatically meant its transformation (Freire 1999b: 102–103).

We can see that the Brazilian educator did not consider conscientization to be an essential part of the process of radical social transformation. This position on the central educational goal of curriculum relates to another position of his on the central political goal of curriculum, that is, the promotion of a militant democracy. The latter was very similar to John Dewey's political goal of education, a fact that should not surprise us if we consider that Freire was influenced by Dewey's ideas and by liberal progressive education in general. Dewey, the most important representative of this school of thought, argued for a widening and deepening of the democratic operation of society without supporting the radical social transformation of all social and political relations and practices.

Progressive education appeared in Brazil during the 1920s and 1930s as a result of industrialization and urbanization. The Brazilian Education Association was founded in 1924, with famous Brazilian educators such as Fernando de Azevedo and Paschoal Lemme among its members. The association promoted an important reform movement, and its ideas were reflected in the constitution of the subsequent decade. The emergent liberal bourgeois elite, inspired by Dewey's North American progressivism and pragmatism, created the New School movement aimed at promoting Brazil's modernization by establishing that schooling must be secular, mandatory, free for all, and an obligation of the state.

The Manifesto of the Pioneers of the New Education, published in 1932, expressed the opinions of the New School representatives who supported the extension of public education, as well as many other innovations that would promote a shift in Brazilian education, favoring an active educational program that would relate school teaching to economic and social reality and dissociating it from old practices. In addition, these ideas propelled Brazilian education in the direction of modernization and democracy through the introduction of vocational education and the development of citizenship in the curricula (O'Cadiz, Wong, and Torres 1998: 18–19; Gadotti 1997: 125).

Anisio Teixeira, descendant of a rich family from Bahia and one of the most important and well-known educators of Brazil, had completed his Ph.D. studies at Columbia University and was an admirer of Dewey's work, which he introduced into Brazil. Teixeira's work (in important official positions of state governments and research centers) focused on fighting elitism, excessive centralism, and bureaucratic policies. The governing ideas of his theoretical work were democracy and economic development through a process of industrialization based on science and societal peace. In his view, knowledge should be a product of experience, creativity, and responsibility achieved through an education oriented toward the future. His most famous work, published in 1957, is *Education Is Not a Privilege*, in which he defended the democratization of teaching (Araujo 1998: 118–119; Gadotti 1994: 171–172).

Freire not only knew Teixeira's views, but he also acknowledged Teixeira's contribution to his own pedagogical ideas and practice. The fact that originally his criticism of the traditional school was inspired by thinkers from the New School did not prevent him from (later) criticizing the very system of capitalism, thus going well beyond the ideas of this democratic movement (Freire 1996a: 89).

Freire believed that an analysis of technologically advanced societies would reveal that human critical ability had been domesticated by a situation where human beings are massified and there is nothing more than the illusion of choice left for them. According to him, mass production as an organization of human labor has become one of the most powerful instruments for the massification of individuals, because they are required to behave mechanically with no critical attitude toward production. Hence, mass production dehumanizes human beings, domesticates them, and, by constricting their horizons, makes them passive, fearful, naïve beings. Here is where the chief contradiction of mass production lies: although it broadens people's sphere of participation, it simultaneously distorts that sphere and, in so doing, eliminates their critical capacity through exaggerated specialization.

Freire dissociated himself from romanticism and its tendency to defend older forms of production. "One cannot solve this contradiction by defending outmoded and inadequate patterns of production, but by accepting reality and attempting to solve its problems objectively. The answer does not lie in rejection of the machine, but rather in the humanization of man" (Freire 1974: 34–35).

In addition to his critical position on the effects of techno-logical and productive modernization, Freire also put forward his positions on the issue of knowledge. Specifically, by analyz-ing the ideas on which his literacy program (launched before 1964) was based, Freire supported the following positions on the knowledge issue:

a. The relation of human beings to reality, expressed as a relation between a subject and an object, results in knowl-edge expressed through language.
b. There is no such thing as absolute ignorance or absolute wisdom.
c. Human beings do not perceive data collected from real-ity in a pure form: as they conceive a phenomenon or a problem, they also conceive its causal links.
d. The more accurately people apprehend true causality, the more critical their understanding of reality will be.
e. Critical consciousness submits this causality to analysis—what is true today may not be so tomorrow (Freire 1974: 43–44).

Freire further explained his rejection of the existence of an absolute ignorance: "The dominating consciousness makes ignorance absolute in order to manipulate the so-called 'uncultured.' If some men are 'totally ignorant,' they will be incapable of managing themselves, and will need the orientation, the 'direction,' the 'leadership' of those who consider themselves to be 'cultured' and 'superior'" (Freire 1974: 43). Indeed, after accumulating experiences in the field of adult education for more than fifteen years in urban and rural proletarian and subproletarian areas, Freire never abandoned the conviction that only by working with the people could he achieve anything authentic.

Therefore, we can understand why the content of Freire's literacy program depended partly on research carried out on generative words, in this way highlighting the program's dependence on basic concepts, ideas, and learner practices that promoted possibilities for discussions about everyday life in social, political, and cultural contexts. In other words, this dependence constituted his departure point for defining the content of the curriculum. His position was founded on his belief in the ontological orientation of *humanization,* his reservations about the consequences of technological and productive modernization, his views on knowledge, and his involvement in MCP. Furthermore, this position related to the popular masses' active participation in the socioeconomic development of Brazil, a development that could and had to depend on these masses. His position did not constitute an attempt to ensure the efficiency of the educational process, which would be defined exclusively by the program associates who were the experts. If the program was not so based, it would lead to the participants being manipulated by a body of experts who would define themselves as superior to the ignorant.

The first phase of the program involved researching the vocabulary of illiterate people coming from urban or rural communities. Lists of words having existential meaning and emotional content were constructed by groups of educators based on their encounters (in some cases) and interviews with members of the group they were working with. The selected words and expressions had to be linked to the participants' experiences, revealing their longings, frustrations, hopes, and impetus to participate.

These lists were to emerge from the educators' vocabulary research, not from their personal inspiration or their previous ideas about illiterates.

During the second phase, a number of generative words were selected according to their syllabic length, their phonetic value, and the social meaning they had for the group. They were called "generative" because of their power to generate or suggest other words for the participants. These words, being highly charged with existential meaning, not only corresponded to participants' basic concepts, ideas, and practices, but they were also capable of generating in people the ability to discuss the social, cultural, and political reality in which they lived. Additionally, these words could generate reflection on participants' lived experiences by providing them with the potential for a deeper and more critical understanding of their reality. Another criterion that had to be met by generative words was their capacity to include basic sounds and a combination of syllables from which, if combined in a different way, new words could be derived.

The creation of codifications (mostly sketches or photographs) comprised the third phase, during which representations of the participants' concrete reality functioned as challenges or, in other words, as coded situation-problems to be decoded and discussed by the participants in cooperation with their educators. These codifications would very often refer to familiar local situations that opened perspectives for the analysis of problems such as nationalism, democracy, development, and literacy. Generative words were set into the codifications, and they could either express the entire situation or refer to only one of its elements.

The fourth and fifth phases of the program involved choosing the content to be taught, as well as the teaching methods to be used for the decoding of the codifications and the participants' acquisition of writing and reading skills. The educator, together with the participants, formed a "cultural circle" (Freire 1974: 42, 49–52).

Preceding the teaching based on generative words, from two to eight hours were devoted to teaching with the use of ten sketches made by Freire's friend and well-known artist Franscisco

Brennand. Through the discussion of the situations depicted in the sketches, which had to be taught in a fixed sequence, participants were introduced to the anthropological concept of culture.

The first sketch shown stimulated a discussion on the primary differences between culture and nature; the sketches that followed illustrated these differences by focusing on several details. Specifically, the negotiation of the situations presented in sketches 2–5 contributed to the participants' understanding of the difference between human beings and animals by focusing on the human abilities to create culture and to communicate. The issue of transforming nature into culture through human mediation was dealt with in sketches 3, 6, and 7. Sketches 2 and 8 were used to examine communication as culture; patterns of behavior and traditions as a cultural manifestation were tackled by means of sketch 9. Sketch 10 initiated discussion on the participants' behavior.

Educators coordinated the discussions on the ten sketches without the use of any written text. The fact that the participants were illiterate did not hinder the study of very complicated themes because the ideas were introduced through graphic representations easily apprehended by the participants. Thus, they were very eager to learn because they were given the opportunity to express what they really knew without being humiliated. Only after an exhaustive analysis of all ten situations were the participants introduced to the first generative word. At the end of that lesson, they had to generate words using a "discovery card,"[5] and on the following day they had to bring from home as many words as they were able to make. The remaining generative words were taught in the lessons to follow, one generative word per lesson. During the literacy program, the participants practiced writing as well as reading aloud, expressed their opinions both in conversation and in writing, studied newspapers, and discussed issues of local interest. Those who completed the literacy lessons were able to read and write simple texts, understand texts in local newspapers, and discuss Brazilian current affairs (Brown 1987: 217, 225, 230).

The National Literacy Program of the Ministry of Education and Culture, which Freire coordinated, did not confine itself to a literacy program. It also planned a postliteracy stage, which would vary only as to content. If the National Literacy Program had not been terminated by the military coup in 1964, there would have been more than twenty thousand culture circles throughout the country whose task would have been to investigate the themes of the Brazilian people. These themes would have been analyzed by specialists and broken down into units, as had been done with the coded situations linked to the generative words. Filmstrips and simplified texts with references to the original texts would have been prepared. By gathering this material, the program would have been able to offer a substantial postliteracy stage. Furthermore, the sphere of the program could have been widened through the creation of a list of thematic breakdowns and bibliographic references to be made available to high schools and colleges (Freire 1974: 56–57).

2

FORMING A PERSPECTIVE FOR
CURRICULUM PLANNING

⤙

THE PEDAGOGY OF THE OPPRESSED

The military coup in Brazil in April 1964 meant persecutions,
exile, and death for many of those who, directly or indirectly,
had supported the attempts for democratization of the country.
According to a report, the military government put forty-six
thousand people in jail, the majority sentenced without charges.
The big landowners, under the protection of the army and the
police, grabbed this long-waited opportunity and eliminated local peasant leaders, many of whom went missing (Frank 1969:
193).

The new government immediately suspended the National
Literacy Program. Those who had taken part in the program
were questioned, accused of making Brazil a Bolshevik country,
and, in many cases, imprisoned. According to a law enacted
nine days after the coup, one hundred popular members of Joao
Goulart's government were deprived of their political rights for
a decade. Paulo De Tarso, minister of education, and the director of the Literacy Program, Paulo Freire were among them.
When the coup took place, Freire was in Brazilia. Soon after,

he was arrested, and his stay in prison lasted seventy-five days, an experience he later considered very useful because "when I was in a box one meter, seventy centimeters long and sixty centimeters in width ... to become free from that envelope I needed something more than my consciousness, and this is the main point to be emphasized" (Jeria 1986: 44–46). These remarks were probably an indirect self-criticism concerning his underestimation of the political preconditions of the social trans-formation process in contrast to the educational work needed for conscientization before 1964. According to one of Freire's close collaborators, during the 1980s Freire's imprisonment experi-ences helped him to clarify the relationship between education and politics and confirmed his thesis that social change would have to come from the masses and not from isolated individuals (Gadotti 1994: 35).

During his period of imprisonment and interrogations (which mainly focused on the political consequences of the Literacy Program), he was dismissed from his teaching post at the Uni-versity of Recife and also lost his position there as the director of the Cultural Extension Service (SEC). The military govern-ment considered him an "international subversive," a "traitor to Christ and the Brazilian people," and it tried to prove that he was "absolutely ignorant and illiterate." As Carmen mentions, the military coup compared his pedagogical methods to those of Joseph Stalin, Adolf Hitler, Juan Perón, and Benito Mussolini (Carmen 1998: 64).

In September 1964, Freire took refuge in the Bolivian Embassy and went to La Paz. Fifteen days after his arrival, he was forced to leave the country due to a military coup there that overthrew the government that had offered him asylum. This time his des-tination was Chile, where a new period of his life would begin, a period we can call the years of exile (1964–1980). Those years were characterized by his adoption of new political ideas intensely influenced by a heterodox interpretation of Marxism. The year 1964 constitutes a decisive shift, a change in the political orienta-tion of the Brazilian educator, that we need to acknowledge in order to examine the second phase of his work.

Immediately after his arrival in Chile, Freire worked as a consultant for Jacques Choncol, an economist, president of the Institute for the Development of Animal Husbandry, and subsequent minister of agriculture in the Salvador Allende's government. While working in what was then termed in Chile "human promotion," Freire was able to extend his collaboration to the Ministry of Education and the people working in adult literacy, as well as to organizations dealing with agrarian reform (Freire 1999b: 34, 39, 51).

A new department specializing in the needs of adult education, independent from the Chilean Ministry of Education, was created. Its mission was to organize courses following the "Freire method" both in rural and urban areas all over the country. It was also to compile material to satisfy the needs of the plan for agrarian reform put in action in 1964 during the presidency of the Christian Democrat Eduardo Frei. The rural reform provided for the abolition of large landownership, known as *latifundios*. In the initial phase, the land laborers were called "settlers" and cultivated the land of *latifundios* on a temporary basis for three years. During this phase, they received assistance from the governmental program of agrarian reform until the day when they would definitely be assigned their own land. Education played an important role in the process of providing assistance to the land laborers (Jeria 1986: 50–51).

According to Austin's analysis, the program of agrarian reform by the Christian Democratic Party (PDC) in Chile can be considered a response partly to modernization pressures from several sources and partly to the increasing influence of certain political organizations on peasants (Movement for Unified Popular Action and the Left Revolutionary Movement), as well as to establishment fears that the peasants would unite with the industrial working class. The Christian Democrats aspired to present their party as a moderate version of Allende's Popular Action Front (FRAP) by promoting the idea of "Chilenization" of industry as the alternative to FRAP's positions on nationalization. As a further alternative to FRAP's socialist revolution, the PDC sought to promote the concept of "revolution in liberty."

The Freirean "psychosocial methodology" that was based on conscientization was put into practice. However, according to Gajardo,[1] the popular education and popular culture movements, after having compromised with the state, were on their way to open antagonism against the hegemony of the dominant classes. They considered education to be an instrument of class struggle for the creation of hegemony in favor of the working classes. In addition, the tension between the conservative Vatican theological doctrine and the rising liberation theology movement in Latin America deepened the contradictions within the Frei regime.

The Christian Left, headed by Choncol, regarded the implementation of Freirean methodology as imperative, especially after the Medellín General Conference of the Latin American Episcopate in 1968.[2] Freire worked for two teams in an institution named ICIRA that studied the agrarian reform in Chile, but he worked mostly with the more radical team, headed by Ronaldo Pinto. In 1968, this team advised him to renounce the PDC reform action plan and to relate to the struggles for popular education that had begun in Chile during the previous century. Eventually, Freire collaborated with the Popular Unity team in ICIRA (Austin 1997: 330, 332–333, 336, 338–339).

Freire's stay in Chile proved to be quite productive because he wrote a series of texts related to rural reform. These texts, together with his essay entitled "Extension or Communication," constituted the second part of a volume published in English with two different titles *Education for Critical Consciousness* and *Education: The Practice of Freedom*. Freire felt they helped "fill possible gaps between *Cultural Action for Freedom* and *Pedagogy of the Oppressed*" (Freire 1985a: xxvii). These writings addressed the need for rural reform in Chile and belonged to the same "family" as *Pedagogy of the Oppressed* and *Cultural Action for Freedom*. Footnotes in his text "Extension or Communication" link it with *Pedagogy of the Oppressed*, something that does not happen in the essay "Education as the Practice of Freedom."

We can see that Freire was bringing together those positions he articulated in Chile and that he considered them to be different from those expressed during his work in Brazil before

44

1964, which, as we saw, were part of *Education: The Practice of Freedom,* even though that book was written in Chile. Additionally, "Extension or Communication" was written in 1968, three years after Freire wrote the essay "Education as the Practice of Freedom" (Goulet 1974: vii). To sum up, the essay "Education as the Practice of Fredom" outlines Freire's theoretical and practical work until 1964, whereas the ideas expressed in *Pedagogy of the Oppressed* introduce a new era in his work.

Years later, Freire pointed out that *Pedagogy of the Oppressed* entailed a radical understanding of his work and that the title of the book was meant to emphasize the existence of a pedagogy carefully hidden in various titles and terms: the pedagogy of the oppressors. He also claimed that one of his objectives while writing it was to direct people's attention to the role to be played by the working classes during their liberation process (Torres and Freire 1994: 102–103).

According to Freire, when he arrived in Chile, only a few days after the inauguration of the Frei government, there was a climate of euphoria in Santiago. It was as if a profound and radical transformation of society had occurred. The Christian Democrat activists were absolutely certain that their revolution was fixed on solid ground because of the "democratic and constitutionalist tradition of the Chilean armed forces." During those days, Freire experienced a rich, problem-fraught process influenced by the climate of accelerated change, with lively discussions taking place in cultural circles where educators often had to beg the peasants to stop after being exhausted with discussions that had gone on all night. He was impressed by the intensity of the peasants' involvement in the analysis of their local and national reality. "It was as if the 'culture of silence' was suddenly shattered, and they had discovered not only that they could speak, but that their critical discourse upon the world, their world, was a way of remaking that world" (Freire 1999b: 34, 38).

As Freire asserted, "Latin America was effervescent in Santiago." The Cubans who were there, even though they felt threatened by the reactionary forces, showed nevertheless that changes could be made. There were guerrilla theories, the "foco" theory but also liberation theology; the charismatic personality of Camilo Torres was there, too, along with Che Guevara's capacity for love.[3] In May 1968, there were the rebellious and libertarian student movements, and also Herbert Marcuse with his influence on youth, while in China there was Mao Zedong and the Cultural Revolution. Santiago had become not only a center for intellectuals and politicians of the most diverse ideas but also the best center for learning in Latin America. There were analyses ranging from an almost unrestricted acceptance of Christian Democracy to its total rejection, as well as sectarian criticism and open and radical criticism in the sense that Freire himself advocated (Freire 1999b: 43–44).

The situation in Chile, as described by Freire, is an example of the influence on his thinking by the ideologico-political theoretical approaches and practices that depended on Marxism. Nonetheless, they were not integrated in the orthodox communist movement, whose stable point of reference was the former Soviet Union and its corresponding version of Marxism-Leninism. Plinio Sampaio, Freire's good friend and collaborator, pointed out that Freire and a number of other exiles gained greater exposure to Marxist class analysis during the Chilean experience, which added a new, significant dimension to his analyses from 1964 onward (Mayo 2004: 12–13). As Austin mentions, Freire, in a paper written in 1991 entitled "I Became 'Almost Chilean,'" points out that in Chile he "learned to learn" (Austin 1997: 324).

Lucio Coletti, drawing mainly from intellectuals whose work was published in the international journal *Monthly Review* in 1967, challenged the model of the revolution in the colonies or the former colonies. This model provided for two phases: (1) the urban-democratic, anti-imperialistic phase, and (2) the socialist phase. Despite this model, the focal point of the world revolution was shifting from the industrial metropolis of the West to the underdeveloped rural areas of Asia and Latin America, in as much as the shining Cuban revolution remained intact despite Che Guevara's death in Bolivia. The Vietnamese were asserting this position and providing arguments of crucial importance. An underdeveloped rural population had not only dared to challenge the world's industrial and military superpower but had also been much admired by the West for making the war a successful issue. The Chinese revolution was projected as an alternative model to the one provided by the Russian Revolution. The latter, begun in the cities, was based on the proletariat, whereas the former, begun in the countryside, was based on the peasants. A popular essay at that time, echoing the positions of the Chinese leadership, concluded that North America and Western Europe could be regarded as the areas where the revolutionary movement of the proletariat had slowed its pace after World War II, whereas Asia, Africa, and Latin America could be regarded as the countryside where the people's revolutionary movement was expanding with robustness and determination (Coletti 1982).

To sum up, a daring and radically new interpretation of Marxism was put forward in both the West and the East during the late 1960s. The working class, the proletariat of the big factory, was no longer the subject of the revolution. The center of the revolution moved from the industrialized countries to the underdeveloped ones, and a new subject began slowly to emerge: the peasants. The proletariat in Western Europe, which Karl Marx considered to be a pioneer in the international revolutionary movement, had actually become a reformist power, which de facto strengthened capitalism. Because Marxism in its entirety was not called into question, the proposed solution was to apply an extended version of Marxist analysis to the universal situation.

Imperialist exploitation led industrialized countries to affluence and the development of the working classes. However, because development and underdevelopment were opposing but also complementary notions, imperialist exploitation was causing increasing poverty and misery among the working classes in the underdeveloped, dependent countries. These masses, functioning as the industrial proletariat described by Marx in the mid-nineteenth century, were becoming the vehicle for revolutionary reform.

These positions criticized the Soviets, focusing mainly on the distance between the mass of the working people and the bureaucratic body of the political leaders, the depoliticization of the masses, urban values and behaviors, and the material motives for the economy. These same positions were also related to the fact that a new class usually emerged initially in the form of a social layer and only after several generations was it established as a class. The Soviet Union's image started to fade, even though neither the Twentieth Soviet Communist Party conference nor de-Stalinization had cast a shadow on it. When conceived as a way to develop productive powers as well as nationalize the means of production, socialism offered preparatory measures that were essential, though utterly insufficient by themselves, to achieve a complete revolution. It was arguable that if the environment was transformed, then people would also be transformed. In the Soviet Union the environment had already been transformed: not only had individual property been abolished, but the country had also been industrialized to a great extent based on public economy.

However, the development of productive powers had neither revolutionized social relations nor transformed people. What seemed to be a possible solution was an educational/cultural revolution. Mao seemed to take advantage of the negative experience in the Soviet Union. Creating a human socialist nature was what really mattered to him. The revolution was not a momentary action; it had to continue for a long historical period so as to eliminate the ethical and ideological legacy of many centuries via class struggle and revolutionary practice. However important were the nationalization of property, the creation of a powerful heavy industry, and the rise in the standards of material life, they did not constitute the central problem of the transition to socialism. The turning point was the transformation of the people. These are the reasons that the Chinese leader embarked upon an educational/cultural revolution.

The outburst of the 1968 incidents intensified the criticism of the Soviet Union and the communist parties in the West. The youth masses of petit-bourgeois origin started to rebel in Berlin, Rome, Milan, and Paris. Despite the confusion apparent in their political slogans, these masses were rebelling against imperialism and were supporting Vietnam using the names of Guevara, Ho Chi Minh, Mao, and Marx, not with a view to some kind of a reform but rather with a view to revolution and communism. The incidents of May 1968 in France were considerably more significant than a simple outburst of the student movement. The youth revolution spread far beyond the student movement, and it was catalytic in calling a general strike involving employees, technicians, tradespeople, and the middle layers, which had remained inactive during the workers' struggles in the past (Coletti 1982: 5–27).

Coletti illustrates the way intellectuals who did not belong to the orthodox communist movement of that period, which was directly influenced by the politics and the ideology of the Soviet Union (in one way or another the orthodox communist movement supported the Soviet Union, considering it to be a socialist country), attempted to form an alternative Left, social, and political strategy, based mainly on the advocacies of dependency theory and the political line of cultural revolution. Coletti's analysis is useful for our understanding of Freire's political positions during his years of exile because, as will be shown later, the Brazilian educator followed a similar direction.

It is not at all accidental that Freire quoted Rosa Luxemborg ("As long as theoretic knowledge remains the privilege of a handful of 'academicians' in the Party, the latter will face the danger of going astray" [cited in Freire 1996b: 21]) when he substantiated his claims about the characteristics of a radical person. According to him, the radical person should not be afraid to see the world unveiled, to meet people, to listen to their opinions, to enter into dialogue with them, or even to confront them. The radical person is not the proprietor of history or of all people, or the liberator of the oppressed; on the contrary, each radical person should commit to fight on the side of the people. In this sense, it is not accidental that Freire decided that the three chapters he had originally written for *Pedagogy of the Oppressed* were not enough and that he needed a fourth chapter (Freire 1999b: 59–60) to refer to issues of political science (Borg and Mayo 2000), with a discussion on revolutionary leadership drawing extensively from Marx, V. I. Lenin, Mao, Fidel Castro, Guevara, Georg Lukács, Louis Althusser, and so on.

Freire formulated a political framework in this book that, according to Torres, was influenced by many philosophical theories: phenomenology, existentialism, Christian personalism, humanist Marxism, and Hegelianism (Torres 1994b: 186–187).[4] His basic ideas could be outlined as follows: the fundamental social contradiction is between the oppressors and the oppressed. For the definition of these terms, the Brazilian educator employed G. W. F. Hegel's definition of the master/slave relationship.[5] The oppressors are independent and exist for themselves, whereas the oppressed are dependent and live and exist for others. The oppressor-oppressed relationship is established on concrete ground and cannot be defined merely as a relationship between different kinds of consciousness. The radical requirement is that this relation must be transformed.

Freire defined the relationship between the oppressors and the oppressed as antagonistic. The concept of class conflict upsets the oppressors, who, being unable to deny the existence of social classes, advocate for understanding and harmony between those who buy and those who are obliged to sell their labor. Nonetheless, the evident antagonism that exists between these two classes makes "harmony" impossible to achieve (Freire 1996b: 21–22, 124–125).

On the basis of this framework, I agree with Peter McLaren and Colin Lankshear, who point out that (a) the objective conditions of oppression are present in *Pedagogy of the Oppressed*, even though the presence of the subject is evident; and (b) the subject is not the same as the one brought forth by various later discourses in the 1990s. The object of the oppression and ideological dominance—subject of the humanizing action of liberation—might not have been identical with the Marxist subject of history, that is, the proletariat, but it was collective, rather than individual, and unifying and coherent, rather than multiple and decentralized (McLaren and Lankshear 1994: 3).

According to Puiggros, the Brazilian educator's basic category of analysis was "people," which was much wider than that of "social class." People, which as a category did not exclude social class, also allowed for the identification of subjects that resulted from multiple articulations between dissimilar elements. The basic characteristic of people as a category of analysis was a theoretical semistructured space, which allowed for the recognition of a certain articulation between subjects; it is a term used by Freire without being accurately defined. A category of analysis very important for the universe of his concepts was people, because it included complex social, cultural, and political subjects. During the 1970s, Freire was criticized by the Left (especially in Brazil) for the use of this term. Leftists underestimated his work because he neither accepted social class as the only theoretical mode for the classification of the population, nor did he consider it to be the only valid dimension of social differentiation (Puiggros 1994: 167–168).

However, as Mayo points out, there are thirty-three references to social class in *Pedagogy of the Oppressed* (Mayo 1997: 6). Freire himself also pointed out that while writing this book, he was trying to analyze the phenomenon of oppression without focusing on oppression suffered because of color, gender, or race, because at that time he was "more preoccupied ... with the oppressed as a social class" (Freire 1997: 309). The Brazilian educator used the term *oppression* as an essential concept in his attempt to define social classes, confusing it with the term *exploitation*. However, according to Lenin, the classic Marxist way of defining social classes was based on the concept of exploitation.

The weakest part of Freire's work is therefore the vagueness of his social analysis. According to Walker, Freire, influenced by Mao Zedong, believed that the peasants had greater revolutionary potential than the working class (Walker 1980: 137–138). Walker's claims are substantial because according to Freire, the proletariat of the cities, although occasionally rebellious, did not have a revolutionary consciousness and considered itself to be privileged, thus becoming an object of manipulation through deceit and promises by the ruling class.

According to the Brazilian educator, revolution can be achieved through praxis, that is, action and reflection directed at the structures to be transformed. The revolutionary effort aiming at the radical transformation of these structures could not possibly consider leaders as its thinkers and the oppressed as its mere activists. The leaders are responsible for coordinating and often directing, but at the same time their action and reflection cannot proceed without the action and reflection of the oppressed. Manipulation, sloganeering, regimentation, and prescription cannot constitute revolutionary praxis precisely because they characterize the oppressors. The validity of any revolution coming from antidialogical action is quite dubious because it may facilitate the creation of a sectarian climate and the subsequent establishment of a bureaucracy, which could undermine the revolution.

There are some well-intentioned—but misguided—men and women who believe that because the dialogical process is protracted, they should carry on with the revolution without the tool of communication, but use instead directives and deem that they will develop a radical educational effort once the revolution has been won. These men and women, however, by denying the feasibility of the leaders' behavior in a critically educational way before taking power, also deny the revolution's educational quality as a cultural action that is to be transformed into a cultural revolution.[6] Because the revolution has an undeniably educational nature, in the sense that unless it liberates, it is not a revolution, the taking of power is only a decisive moment in the revolutionary process. When the revolution is viewed as dynamic, there is no absolute before or after, with the dividing line being the taking of power. If it was impossible to dialogue with the people before the taking of power because they were inexperienced in dialoguing, it would then be impossible for the people to come into power because they are equally inexperienced in exercising power. This educational-dialogical quality is one of the most effective instruments for keeping the revolution from being hemmed in by a counterrevolutionary bureaucracy (Freire 1996b: 106–111, 130–133, 148–152).

Although Freire's contract with the ICIRA program came to an end in 1969, due to its success, it seemed likely to be extended. However, he did not receive a new offer, probably because, as a consultant for the United Nations attached to the

ICIRA program contended, "political motives may have had some influence in the termination of Freire's employment at ICIRA" (Jeria 1986: 49, 53). Both Jeria and Austin point out that there were several debates within the Christian Democrats on the underlying ideas of the literacy program (Jeria 1986; Austin 1997). Freire indirectly confirms their views, saying that his work in ICIRA coincided with the first condemnations lodged against him by the extreme right-wing sectors of the Christian Democrats in Chile for things he had never done nor would ever do (Freire 1999b: 51).

After enjoying international recognition,[7] Freire co-operated with the Study Center for Education and Development at Harvard University and a study center in Cuernavaca, Mexico, that was directed by Ivan Illich. According to a report from a meeting held in Mexico (the central speakers were Freire, the Protestant theologian Ruben Alves, and the Bolivian communist Ramiro Reynaga) in 1970, Freire ardently argued that socialism was the only social organization that could humanize. Education for liberation could help people become aware that the existing social organization was to blame for their current position, if there was blame to be had, and that only socialism would help them to solve their problems (Collins 1973: 38).

During that period he wrote two papers, published in the *Harvard Educational Review*.[8] He was also in conversation with the World Council of Churches (WCC) in Geneva about the possibility of working there as a consultant in the education department. In January 1970, he left Harvard to join the WCC program in Geneva. This was the first time a non-Protestant took on such a prominent role in the WCC (Jeria 1986: 53–54). It was very important for him, as he later explained to his friends when leaving Santiago, to pass through the "center of capitalist power" because he needed to see "the animal close up in its home territory." As for his decision to accept WCC's proposal rather than Harvard's proposal to teach there, he explained that WCC was giving him the opportunity to travel the world, expose himself to various environments, learn of other people's experiences, and take a fresh look at himself through cultural differences, thus overcoming the risk that exiles sometimes run of being too remote from the most concrete experiences. Working with WCC could also help him avoid becoming lost in a game of words (Freire and Faundez 1992: 12–13).

EDUCATION AND SOCIALIST TRANSFORMATION

A proposal made by the Guinea-Bissau government gave him the opportunity to come back to the literacy field. The Institute for Action and Conscientization (IDAC), which was formed within the framework of WCC, proposed an educational program that included Cape Verde, Guinea-Bissau, Angola, and São Tomé. Many Brazilian educators, sociologists, and linguists, Freire and his wife, Elza, among them, participated. The work in Guinea-Bissau lasted from 1975 to mid-1978 (Jeria 1986: 55) and resulted in Freire's book *Pedagogy in Process: The Letters to Guinea-Bissau*.

Between 1975 and 1978, the Brazilian educator worked in São Tomé, not as a specialist consultant but as a militant educator. The revolutionary leadership of this country, which had recently been released from the Portuguese colonial yoke, gave him confidence and proposed that he should develop a literacy program. The results were impressive, much better than expected. Four years later, the minister of education sent Freire a letter saying that 55 percent of all those enrolled and 72 percent of those who had completed the course had become literate (Gadotti 1994: 47).

Guinea-Bissau is a rural country in West Africa smaller than the size of Switzerland, with a population of eight hundred thousand inhabitants. The hard struggles of the African Party for the Liberation of Guinea and Cape Verde (PAIGC), with Amilcar Cabral in charge, managed to counteract the violence of the colonizers, who proved to be incapable of destroying the country schools, the mobile medical stations, or the "people's stores" that thrived in the liberated areas. Even Cabral's assassination in 1973 did not hinder the revolutionary struggle from culminating in a declaration of independence in September 1973 (Darcy de Oliveira and Darcy de Oliveira 1976: 5–6).

Liberation from the colonizers, economic development, establishment of democracy, and construction of a coherent national identity were among the aims of PAIGC, which was fighting for a profoundly democratic revolutionary process. Importantly, Cabral repeatedly warned PAIGC of the dangers of creating an indigenous elite that would simply substitute for the Portuguese colonizers. As far as the party was concerned, the change it was fighting for had to be intrinsically cultural. The cultural transformation could be realized only if men and women engaged in their own spiritual struggles. Cabral used to point out that the rural masses had to undergo a difficult transition from the world of tradition, religion, and magic, to that of thought and political revolution (Stefanos 1997: 247–249).

There were several problems with the literacy program in Guinea-Bissau, the most important being, according to Freire, the language of instruction. There were contradictory views on the issue among the members of the revolutionary government. Freire was in favor of using Creole.[9] However, the view that was eventually adopted was to use Portuguese as the language of instruction because it was considered to be a more complete and richer language.

The language of instruction is an issue with which Freire dealt again some time later while writing *Literacy: Reading the Word and the World* (published in 1987) with Donaldo Macedo. Freire decided to include a letter he had chosen not to include in *Pedagogy in Process*. The letter, addressed to Mario Cabral, commissioner on educational matters and appointed by the government of Guinea-Bissau, was also included in another book of his entitled *Learning to Question: A Pedagogy of Liberation* (a dialogue between Freire and the Chilean philosopher Antonio Faundez published in 1992).

In the letter Freire points out that when a society decides the language of its colonizers should become the language of instruction just immediately after it has freed itself from the colonial yoke, then, wittingly or unwittingly, that choice will likely widen the gap among the country's social classes rather than overcome it. "I could have added in the letter that it would be possible to predict today more or less, in whose hands power will be tomorrow, possibly once again in the hands of an urban *petite bourgeoisie,* perhaps speaking one of the national languages, and Creole, but also having a command of Portuguese. Today children with a command of Portuguese have a clear advantage in school over those who do not, [that is] over workers' children, both urban and rural" (Freire and Faundez 1992: 110).[10]

Freire still held these views four years after having returned to his country following an amnesty granted to him by the military government of Brazil in 1979.[11] (I shall refer to the amnesty in detail in the next chapter.) Freire's warning to Cabral about the consequences of selecting the language of the colonizers as the language of instruction proved to be a major pedagogical concern of his during the 1964–1980 period when he formed a pedagogy that was authentically revolutionary and liberating.

As Freire declared, this line of thought was closely related to that of transcending the naïveté that had characterized his work before 1964. The experience of the military coup seemed to have played a crucial role. While delivering a speech for a UNESCO international symposium on literacy, held in Persepolis in 1976, Freire referred to the naïve belief in the power of institutionalized education to transform reality. He was criticized by some, no less naïve people that even he himself shared this assumption. Nonetheless, Freire maintained, education does not transform society. On the contrary, society, according to its structure, shapes education in terms of the needs and interests of those in power.

The creation of bourgeois education by the bourgeoisie when it is already in power demonstrates that no society can be organized on the basis of its actual educational system. Educational systems have been created and re-created by the social practices that constitute a given society. The role of systematic education in an oppressive society, from which it stems and on which it acts as an agent of social control, is the maintenance of that society.

Consequently, to perceive systematic education as an instrument of liberation is tantamount to giving it an autonomous capacity for transforming society, which is illusionary. In reality, Freire believed, systematic education is not autonomous. Those who work on critically examining these illusions are anything but pessimistic. Clarity of perception that comes from examining the dynamic relations among society, education, and conscious action leads us to discover the functions and the different (but interconnected) modes of education corresponding to the different (but interconnected) moments of the liberation process.

Through lucid observation, we can more or less set the limits of our pedagogical action within the educational system. That the educational system does not constitute an agent of social transformation does not necessarily deny the importance of making concrete efforts within the system. These efforts can be very difficult, but they are not useless (Freire 1976: 196–197).

Given when *Pedagogy of the Oppressed* was written, we can see that it referred to educational projects, not to the curriculum of the official educational network. Freire will deal with problems relating to the curriculum of official education some years later, and they will be analyzed mainly in *Pedagogy in Process,* where the political goal of the education supported by Freire will become much more explicit. In Guinea-Bissau, Freire faced the task of transforming education by approaching it as an educator-consultant of the liberating movement that was in power, rather than as an educator attempting to theoretically construct and implement a revolutionary pedagogy that could not be fully executed in the official educational system, as it was described in *Pedagogy of the Oppressed.*

Freire's main political theses on the relationship between education and sociopolitical transformation are included in *Pedagogy in Process* and can be outlined as follows: the radical transformation of the educational system inherited from the colonizers requires a plan consistent with sociopolitical transformation and has to be based on certain material conditions, including increasing production and its reorientation based on a new concept of distribution. Discussions on what to produce, how to produce it, why, and for whom must be characterized by a high degree of political clarity. Any change, however timidly it is initiated, regarding the new material conditions, such as the dichotomy between manual labor and intellectual labor, provokes resistance from the old ideology that survives. An effort toward massive change at the infrastructure level requires simultaneous ideological action. Furthermore, it entails the reorganization of the means of production as well as the participation of workers in a specific method of education through which, after understanding the process of production itself, they will acquire specific skills.

In his analysis of PAIGC's plan, based on texts published by the government commissioner, Freire commented positively on the importance given to the gradual academic education of students. Such an education would result in an increased understanding of reality as students acted on that reality and came to recognize the necessary relationship between education and production; they would meanwhile be prevented from identifying education with scientism (which mystifies science) as well as from mystifying production and consumerism. One of the basic aspects of the new education system in Guinea-Bissau was that students were invited to develop solidarity and social responsibility, to consider work as a source of knowledge, and to achieve an authentic camaraderie, instead of the competition favored by individualism, in the process of producing what was socially necessary.

According to Freire, this aspect of the new education system related to the students' scientific formation. Furthermore, when a society seeks to live the radical unity between theory and practice, it overcomes the dichotomy between manual labor and intellectual labor, which results in a totally different mode of education. The school—at the primary, secondary, or tertiary level—does not have to be essentially different from the factory or the farm, nor does it have to be in opposition to either. When a school exists outside factory and farm, this does not necessarily mean that it is superior to them, nor does it mean that factory or agricultural work is not school. School cannot be defined as an institution bureaucratically responsible for the transfer of a selected kind of knowledge. Rather, it is a pole or a moment in the unity between theory and practice.

If a society moves toward socialism, it needs to organize its production in terms of this goal; it also needs to structure its education system to understand the productive process and the technical training of learners. The education of laborers in capitalist societies does not offer a total understanding of the productive process. In this context, the creation of a "new man" and a "new woman" can be achieved only by their participating in productive labor that serves the common good. If labor is the source of knowledge, then such education cannot be elitist because it does not lead to a strengthening of the division between manual and mental labor. The struggle for liberation continues even after the people gain political power that constitutes a "cultural fact and a factor of culture" (a phrase used by Amilcar Cabral cited in Freire 1978: 112).

It is quite contradictory for a society, while seeking to reconstruct itself along socialist lines, to become fascinated by the myth of consumerism. If it moves in this direction, its objective will be to produce salable goods, even though it lacks a capitalist class. Socialism, however, is something very different from "a capitalist society without capitalists" (Freire 1978: 108). In a society reconstructed in a revolutionary way, the accumulated capital that is not paid to workers in the form of salary or wages needs to be used for the development of collectivity and the production of goods that are socially necessary and not necessarily salable. This society renounces both the tendency to leave everything to chance and the hardening of bureaucracy. It is founded on a balanced economic development of both primary and secondary production, and it does not consider agriculture to be the servant of industrial production. With a powerful agricultural production, farmers and urban industrial workers will produce for the benefit and well-being of the whole society.

In such a society, if profit continues to have as prominent a role as in a capitalist economy, then production will be oriented toward the values of exchange and not of use. Thus, it will not be surprising that the stimulus will always be of a material nature, which, however, is inconsistent with an educational program linked to production, seeking to build such social incentives as cooperative work and concern for the common good—in other words, an educational program that has a critical belief in the ability of people to be remade in the process of social reconstruction (Freire 1978: 14–15, 46, 77–78, 90, 105, 109, 139–140).

According to Mayo, the existence of a strong relationship between education and production, which was emphasized in Freire's book *Pedagogy in Process,* marked a notable development in his theory, making the social relations of production his focus of attention. Freire's view that there should be no dichotomy between productive labor and education calls to mind a series of Marxist suggestions, such as Marx's 1866 proposal for a polytechnic education and Mao's interchange process of two months of work/four months of study in the Chinese educational system. Mao's system was based on the principle that there is no other way to learn a subject except by practicing it in its own environment (Mayo 2004: 61–62, 68–69). Giroux mentions that Freire's ideas as presented in *Pedagogy in Process* might have cost him his liberal supporters because his attack on the division between work and schooling aimed at radical reconstruction and was not simply liberal rhetoric. After the publication of this book, it would have been difficult for anyone to misinterpret the political assumptions underpinning Freire's theory and practice (Giroux 1981: 135).

Freire's political goal of curriculum planning during this period was radical sociopolitical transformation with a socialist orientation. In *Pedagogy of the Oppressed,* he was quite vague about the content of this revolutionary transformation. He was explicit only in maintaining that the revolution involved popular forces coming into power, as well as a radical change in social structures. He distanced himself from liberal ideas on the issue of the relationship between education and sociopolitical transformation. Specifically, he did not believe that radical sociopolitical transformation could be realized exclusively through a change in people's consciousness absent a transformation of the social and political power structures. Furthermore, he disagreed with overemphasizing the power of education against the power of exploitation.[12]

Freire clarified the content of the sociopolitical transformation he had in mind in *Pedagogy in Process,* where he outlined his positions on the nature of a socialist society. In this way he filled, to a great extent, the gaps in the ideas he presented in *Pedagogy of the Oppressed.*[13] Freire's educational goal of curriculum planning was the same as in his literacy program in Brazil before 1964, when he endorsed the formation of critical consciousness deriving from a conscientization process. According to Freire, whether before the change of political power or after it, conscientization was essential because the revolutionary process was continual and its cultural dimension was critical. The relationship between the leaders of the revolution and the popular masses described in *Pedagogy of the Oppressed* and his positions on how to face the danger of bureaucratization of social transformation included in *Pedagogy in Process* demonstrate that the formation of critical consciousness deriving from a conscientization process was Freire's central educational goal, even when he did not expressly refer to it in his texts after 1974.[14] One example can be drawn from *Pedagogy in Process.* He argued that no increase in production would be possible unless the masses had been involved in the process of political conscientization. This process would serve a different political goal from that of militant democracy (the goal of radical sociopolitical transformation) supported by Freire before 1964. In other words, conscientization was in need of new content.

In *Pedagogy of the Oppressed,* Freire argued that the oppressed need to understand the reality of their oppression, not as a secluded world with no way out but rather as a situation that they can change. Conscientization is the driving force for liberating action, and it also constitutes the necessary, but not adequate, condition for liberation. Freire distinguishes between two forms of consciousness, which are radically different from the three stages of the conscientization process (semi-intransitive consciousness, naïve transitive consciousness, critical transitive consciousness) on which his pre-1964 literacy program was based. He calls the first form of consciousness "real consciousness" and implies the impossibility for an individual of perceiving the "untested feasibility" that lies beyond "limit-situations"; he calls the second form "potential consciousness." His term *limit-situations* refers to those situations that individuals can be caught up in as well as those situations containing actual limits from which potentialities can arise. Untested feasibility can be achieved through a "testing action" and is related to real consciousness; testing action itself is related to potential consciousness (Freire 1996b: 33–34, 94).[15]

As I have written elsewhere, at the end of the 1960s Freire continued to use the term *conscientization,* elaborating the characteristics of the aforementioned three stages. However, his development of this concept through these three stages, which Freire himself had previously considered a critical educational effort based on favorable historical conditions, was placed in a different context. The processes of humanization, of social transformation, and of the formation of a revolutionary pedagogy constituted a new context for conscientization that also gave it new content. Conscientization was a way of approaching the world based on the collective criticism of experienced situations and on the attempt to overcome them. A reading of *Pedagogy of the Oppressed* confirms this.

Freire's attention gradually focused on criticism of oppression in terms of ontology; comprehension of the internalizing of oppression using sociopsychological approaches; criticism against banking education; promotion of the process of posing problems; definition of the preconditions and the features of pedagogical dialogue in the fields of theory and practice; and, finally, criticism of influential political-pedagogical practices favored by the Left. We can see that the main goal of that book was to contribute to the formation of a revolutionary pedagogy (Grollios et al. 2002: xl–xlii).

It can be argued that the meaning of conscientization in Freire's "Education as the Practice of Freedom" is different from the meaning of the same term in *Pedagogy of the Oppressed.* In the former, Freire considered the term as describing a process of three stages. Transformation of consciousness was not related to social or political controversies, being completely cut off from a transformation of the entirety of social and political relations and practices. Conscientization was the exclusive outcome of either socioeconomic modernization or the influence of education.

In *Pedagogy of the Oppressed*, the term was directly related to the issues of oppression and liberation. It was a way of apprehending social reality and a struggle for its transformation by the people, which involved the transition from real consciousness to potential consciousness. This transition constituted an act of liberation, which could be realized only when individuals are active and surpass the limits set by the limit-situations.

Given that for Freire in the period between 1964 and 1980 the political goal to be accomplished through curriculum planning was radical sociopolitical transformation with a socialist orientation, and the educational goal was the formation of critical consciousness as a liberating act promoting the realization of this political goal, we can now direct our attention to the question of defining the content of the curriculum. However, to address this question, we need to look at the basic positions on which Freire's theory on knowledge was based, a theory he put forward mainly during his years of exile (1964–1980). Indeed, most systematic approaches (an outline of which will be provided) to Freire's theory of knowledge, as well as the less systematic ones,[16] refer almost exclusively to works of that period.

THE CONTENT AND PROCESS OF CURRICULUM PLANNING

According to Matthews, Freire's theory of knowledge is the focal point of his pedagogy because it emerges from his personal experiences of acquiring and transmitting knowledge. Even though Freire was not a systematic philosopher, his epistemology presumably constitutes the most developed part of his theory, which consisted of comments, analyses, suggestions, and reflections.

Freire's theory of knowledge was almost the same as that of the young Marx; it shared all his strong and weak points, opposing positivists and idealists who suggested apolitical, nonpractical explanations of human knowledge. Freire supported the view that knowledge stems from the process of reflection on activities performed by active subjects during the transformation of their natural and social worlds. Knowledge is profoundly related to praxis that is social and oriented toward a goal: human liberation and the emancipation of those who are trapped in the culture of silence. Thus, public knowledge is an arena for political struggles to be fought and moral choices to be tested.

Freire's basic positions were these:

a. The activity of knowledge constitutes a work of subjects.
b. There exists a world independent of people, which constitutes the object of mental conceptualization.
c. Mental understanding of the world is determined by needs and interests.
d. Humanized nature and culture become the object of human knowledge, and thus the power of the latter to define is recognizable—the structures of thought should be seen in historical terms and not as innate and nonsocial.
e. Thought has a social, rather than a private-individual, character.
f. There are naïve and refined processes of representation of phenomena, direct and theoretical.
g. The basic function of thought is to secure distance from the object of knowledge, which constitutes a part of the reflective aspect of praxis.
h. Thought is dependent on the revelation of real problems and needs, and the way in which this knowledge is acquired cannot be separated from how it is imparted.
i. Knowledge of objects is knowledge of their relationships, knowledge of the association of one part to the whole within a historical basis.
j. The aim of knowledge is the activity that will lead to humanization through the restructuring of oppressive structures (people belong to societies that have a history, a history of class struggles and struggles of power).

k. Knowledge can never be complete (this position does not lead to relativism or skepticism but rather falls within a developmental, dialectic, and dynamic view of reality) (Matthews 1980: 82–92).

According to Elias, there is a theory of knowledge at the core of Freire's educational philosophy; this theory is evident from his earliest works to his last dialogues. In the framework of Freire's theory, knowing is closely related to consciousness, to becoming aware of the world, ourselves, and our knowledge; both of these are social practices and are connected to the real world. In his early discussions of knowledge, he is under the influence of existentialist thought; in his later work, he is influenced by phenomenologists and especially by Marxists. His rather complex and abstract theory of human knowing includes three main points. First, knowledge comes from the real world. Second, knowledge distinguishes us from animals by enabling us to shape culture and history. Third, although knowledge is culturally bound, if people want to reach critical consciousness, they have to participate in an intentional mode of education based primarily on dialogue. The nature of the dialectical relationship in knowledge between being informed by reality and forming reality is specified in terms of people overcoming the limit-situations of domination and oppression. The most important kind of knowing or coming to critical consciousness occurs when people become aware of oppression and attempt to overcome it through a "knowing struggle" (Elias 1994: 61–62).

Drawing from Matthews and Elias, we can argue that there is a shift in Freire's philosophical thought toward Marxism from 1964 onward. After having presented his basic political positions and his knowledge theory, I will describe his positions on how to define the content of the curriculum, the process of curriculum planning, and the role of the subjects involved in this process.

As discussed in the previous chapter, Freire's definition of the content of the literacy program before 1964 was based, in part, on participants' concepts, ideas, and practices, which offered the possibility for discussions of everyday life in a social, political, and cultural context. Generative words resulted from the researching of people's daily lives. In *Pedagogy of the Oppressed,* this position is expressed in a similar way and is supported in a direct political manner. Freire criticized the revolutionary leaders for espousing a banking approach to constructing the content of a curriculum from top to bottom, thus offering workers or farmers programs relevant to their worldview but not the people's worldview.

To support this view, Freire quoted Mao: "There are two principles here: one is the actual needs of the masses rather than what we fancy they need, and the other is the wishes of the masses, who must make up their own minds instead of our making up their minds for them." To further illustrate his point, Freire quoted Mao again: "We must teach the masses clearly what we have received from them confusedly" (Freire 1996b: 75, 74). Freire believed that this declaration comprised an entire dialogical theory on how to construct the content of education without exclusive dependence on what the educator thinks best for the students. The curriculum content should not be thought of as a gift or as something imposed but rather as an organized, systematized, and developed representation of the things learners wish to learn about.

Language and thought cannot exist outside a structure that frames them. Educators must understand the structural conditions where language and thought take shape. For the curriculum content to be decided, educators need to investigate reality, which mediates people and the perception of that reality held both by educators and the people. Hence, the thought/language used by people to negotiate reality, the levels at which they perceive that reality, and their view of the world constitute the source for the program content or, in other words, the generative themes on which the program content has to be based. The generative themes are closely connected with limit-situations and have the potential to connect with a wide array of other themes. As soon as human beings perceive these limit-situations as fetters, as obstacles to their liberation, they will realize their true nature within concrete historical dimensions of a given reality. Human beings respond to the challenge of these confines by resorting to borderline acts directed at negating and overcoming, rather than passively accepting, these restrictions. These reactions can be achieved only through action upon concrete reality, one where such limit-situations are historically found.

An epoch is characterized by ideas, concepts, hopes, doubts, values, and challenges in dialectical interaction with their opposites. They constitute the themes of that epoch and entail others that are antithetical. They are never isolated, independent, disconnected, or static; rather, they are always interacting with their opposites. The thematic universe of an epoch comprises a complex of these interacting themes.

Generative themes are located in concentric circles, moving from the general to the particular. The broadest epochal unit includes themes of a universal character in a diversified range of units and subunits—continental, regional, national, and so on. For example, the theme of domination, directly related to that of liberation, is, according to Freire, a theme of universal character. Within the smaller concentric circles, one can find themes and limit-situations that are characteristic of societies that share historical similarities. For example, underdevelopment (and the corresponding relationship to dependence) represents a confining characteristic of societies of the so-called Third World. In addition to universally, continentally, or historically similar themes, any society in the broader epochal unit contains its own particular themes and limit-circumstances. Within even smaller circles, one can find thematic diversifications of the same society, which can constitute epochal subunits. For example, the contradiction of the coexistence of the contemporaneous and the noncontemporaneous can be found within the same national unit.

Including the people in the investigation of their generative themes neither falsifies the findings nor sacrifices the objectivity of the investigation because themes are not things and they do not exist in "original objective purity" outside of people. The given fact, the perception that the people have of this fact, and the generative themes arising from it are all related to one another. The aspirations, the motives, and the objectives implicit in the list of important themes do not simply exist somewhere as static entities; rather, they occur. They are as historical as humans are and thus cannot be apprehended separate from them. Consequently, thematic investigation can become a common effort toward awareness of reality and of the self, as well as becoming a starting point for the educational process.

The investigation of these themes will become profoundly educational if it is critical, if it avoids the narrow descriptions of partial views of reality, and if it focuses on the comprehension of material reality. Therefore, the process of investigation for meaningful themes should be characterized by a concern for finding the links between them, for posing them as problems, and for analyzing their historical-cultural context. Every thematic investigation that deepens historical awareness is truly educational. The more educators and people investigate people's thought, the more they continue to investigate. Education and thematic investigations are different moments of the same process. Opposing the antidialogical and noncommunicative deposits of the banking educational method, the curriculum content corresponding to the problem-posing educational method can be selected and organized based on the students' view of the world, where they are encouraged to find their own generative themes. In this way, the content constantly expands and renews itself. The task of dialogical educators in interdisciplinary groups working on the thematic universe is to represent that universe to the people it came from, framing it not as a lecture but as a problem (Freire 1996b: 74–84, 87–90).

As in Freire's literacy project in Brazil before 1964, the process of curriculum planning was not carried out by collaborators (researchers, educators) and experts excluding the people it was designed for. That the program was based on the participants' conceptions of social reality, on their own worldview, constituted the departure point for the definition of curriculum content. Before 1964, Freire had already been paying attention to this process, but after 1964 he became much more interested in it, given that there was no substantial difference between the participants' concepts, ideas, and practices that offered the possibility for discussion on everyday life in a social, political, and cultural context and the participants' conceptions of social reality.

However, the process of curriculum planning described and analyzed in *Pedagogy of the Oppressed,* influenced by his work in Chile, was much more complex and sophisticated, because it was placed in a new political context and a much more comprehensive theory of knowledge. Moreover, people had a much more active participation in this process.

According to Rivera, Freire was influenced by a version of structuralism that differed from the dominant version. While planning his literacy project, Freire spoke about structures of dependency, analyzed epochal themes in terms of these structures of dependency, and contended that people should be made aware of the role that these structures played in their everyday life. The crucial difference between Freire and mainstream structuralists was that the latter were not concerned with the interests of the people they studied; the official version of structuralism was not interested in the emancipation of poor people. Freire's version not only took their interests into account, but it also made the emancipation of poor people its central concern (Rivera 2004: 110–111, 148–149).

In *Pedagogy of the Oppressed,* Freire describes the process of curriculum planning for his adult literacy program. Once the investigators have become acquainted with the area in which they will work through secondary sources, they start the first phase of the investigation. They organize a first contact during which they inform the participants of the reason for the investigation, the way it will be conducted and used, and their objectives; they call for volunteers who will serve as assistants. Meanwhile, the investigators visit the area, acting as sympathetic observers. They perceive the whole area as an enormous, unique, living code to be deciphered by regarding it as a totality to be analyzed in its partial dimensions, thus expanding their understanding of the way these partial dimensions interact. The investigators either observe directly or guide informal conversations with the inhabitants, including almost every dimension of their social life—the way the people talk, their behavior at church and at work; the role played by women and by young people; the way they spend their leisure time, participate in sports, and play games;

the relationships between husband and wife and between parent and child.

Then the investigators and the assistants take part in successive evaluation meetings where they expose, discuss, and reconsider their observations so that they recompose the totality they have observed. The more the team divides and reintegrates the whole, the more they approach the nuclei of the contradictions in which the inhabitants of the area are involved. By tracing these nuclei of contradictions, the investigators can organize the curriculum content of their educational action because if this content reflects the contradictions in that area, then it will certainly contain the meaningful regional themes.

In the second phase, the investigators select some of these contradictions in order to develop the codifications to be used in the thematic investigation. The codifications are objects (sketches, photographs, or some words that pose a problem) whose selection or construction is guided by certain principles different from the ones used to make visual aids. These principles consist of (a) representing situations familiar to the participants so that they can recognize the situations and their relationship to them; (b) forming the thematic nucleus in such a way that it will neither be too explicit, degenerating into propaganda, nor too enigmatic; (c) organizing the codifications like a thematic fan that opens up in the direction of other themes so that the dialectical relations that exist between the themes and their opposites can be perceived by the participants as a totality; and (d) representing contradictions that include other contradictions and hence constitute the system of contradictions for the area under study.

In the third phase, the investigators return to the area under study to initiate dialogue in the thematic investigation circles, each one of which should have a maximum of twenty persons. There should be as many circles as necessary to satisfy the needs of one-tenth of the population of the area under study. The discussions on the codifications are recorded and analyzed by an interdisciplinary team, including volunteers who assisted in the first phases of the investigation and some participants in the thematic investigation circles. Their participation creates the opportunity for the interpretations of the investigation's specialists to be rectified or ratified if needed. During these meetings, the investigators-coordinators must not simply be present; rather, they must present the codified existential situation and their answers to the participants as problems so that they can externalize their feelings and their opinions about themselves, the world, and others, which they might not do in different circumstances. A psychologist and a sociologist also attend the meetings and record the significant (and seemingly insignificant) reactions.

In the fourth phase, the investigators proceed to an interdisciplinary study of their findings, and they subsequently list the themes expressed explicitly or implicitly during the sessions. The themes are classified according to the social sciences they are related to. This does not necessarily mean they are viewed as belonging to isolated categories; rather, a theme can be viewed by each of the social sciences to which it is related. For example, the theme of development can be viewed as relating to economics and also sociology, anthropology, social psychology, or even political science and education.

In this way, the themes belonging to a totality are not examined as rigidly defined concepts; at the same time, the richness of their interpenetration with other aspects of reality is illuminated. While deciding upon the meaningful themes to be dealt with in curriculum content, the team may decide to include some fundamental themes that were not directly suggested by the people. The introduction of these themes, which Freire called "hinged themes," corresponds to the dialogical character of education. Hinged themes either facilitate the connection between the themes, or they illustrate the relationships between the curriculum content and the people's views of the world.

Once the themes to be included in the curriculum content are fixed, each specialist presents to the interdisciplinary team a plan for how each theme will be broken down into learning units, and each also looks for the nuclei through which a general view of the theme will be given. The other specialists make suggestions that can be incorporated into the curriculum and/or included in the brief essays that are written on the theme and that, along with the bibliography provided, are to be used during the training of the teachers who will work in the "culture circle."

The phase of codification follows that of the thematic breakdown. During this fifth phase, the best channel of communication (visual, tactile, audio, or a combination of all) for each theme and its representation is selected. This selection depends on the material as well as on the level of literacy of the participants. Upon completion of the codification, the didactic material is prepared (photographs, slides, filmstrips, posters, reading texts, theatrical performance, etc.). With all the didactic material prepared, the team of educators is ready to present to the people their own thematics in systematized and expanded form. In this manner the themes that have come from the people are returned to them as problems to be solved (Freire 1996b: 91–104).

Without losing the vision of the total plan for the society, educators should keep in mind local conditions of the area where the literacy and postliteracy projects are to begin. The more general situation needs to be understood on the basis of local conditions. Thus, every generative word has to make possible an analysis that would start with the local and would extend to the regional, national, continental, and, eventually, universal. Let us take the generative word *rice* as an example. It is a word of indisputable significance for Guinea-Bissau; the rich theme to which it refers can be the basis for the selection and organization of the curriculum content for adult literacy education as well as for postliteracy programs of primary and secondary levels. Freire, referring neither to all the thematic areas associated with the generative word in question nor to its rigorous ordering of sequence, would give examples of thematic areas (production, geography, politics, history, health) and also would point out that they needed to be studied by a national interdisciplinary team. This team would base its work on the social plan and the political principles of the party and the government. The themes included would become topics for debate among the learners, who would make their contribution to the organization of the program content of their own education. The participants in the cultural circles would play an active role in the collection of local data related to the generative theme. For example, the peasants in Chile carried out projects making a sociocultural diagnosis of their communities and were also responsible for the presentation of these data (Freire 1978: 100–104, 112–120).

Freire argued that any attempts to define the content of curriculum should be made in reference to social context (which was a political issue and thus the experts should not be left aside). He clarified this notion in his article "The People Speak Their Word" about his literacy project in São Tomé, which was published in 1981 in the *Harvard Educational Review*. In this article Freire stressed that the *Popular Culture Notebooks*, basic books for learners both in the initial and follow-up phases of learning to read and write, were neither textbooks or exercise books with manipulative texts nor neutral books. The opposite of manipulation is neither the illusion of neutrality nor the illusion of spontaneity; instead, it is the critical and democratic participation of the learners in the act of knowing, of which they are the subjects.

The fundamental themes associated with the majority of generative words that constitute the content of this literacy project relate both to the understanding of the dynamics of labor (the complex phenomenon of productivity, the way production is organized and developed, the need to train workers without confining them to a narrow and alienating specialization) and to the understanding of culture, its role in the liberation and national reconstruction processes, and the problem of defining one's own cultural identity without naïvely rejecting the contribution of any other culture. These themes are discussed at an introductory level in the initial phase of learning to read and write, and they are presented as problems in the *Popular Culture Notebooks* during the follow-up stage (Freire 1981: 28–29).

3

REFORMING THE CURRICULUM
IN SÃO PAULO

‑๑‑

THE WORKERS PARTY

In December 1979, the military government of Brazil enforced a law granting amnesty to hundreds of academics, civil servants, and military personnel. This law allowed all these people to be reinstated in the posts they had occupied before the military coup (Jeria 1986: 58–59).

Freire's return to his country meant the beginning of a new period in both his life and his work. After having spent sixteen years in exile, he had to relearn his homeland, which differed a lot from the country he had left in 1964. Further developments in the mid-1980s led to the destabilization of the military coup and to the restoration of democracy. Freire was actively involved in these developments through his affiliation with a new political party, the Workers Party (PT), whose creation was integrally related to the struggles for the democratization of Brazil.

The political positions in the third and final period of Freire's work are better understood only after an analysis of the basic characteristics of PT, which played such an important role in Brazilian politics. As Freire explained, it was the first time he had become a member of a political party; he did so because PT was the first party to have been born "from down up ... not rejecting the so-called intellectuals for being intellectuals, but rejecting elitist and authoritarian intellectuals for claiming ownership over the truth of the working class and of the revolution." According to one of his statements, he had "waited for more than forty years for the Workers Party to be created" (Freire 1993b: 57, 139).

At the beginning of 1980, twelve hundred people gathered in São Paulo to take the first steps in the creation of PT. It was officially founded four months later, in June 1980, when its declaration was signed. Among its founding members were several renowned leftists, intellectuals, and the most popular leaders of the so-called new union movement. PT's manifesto stated: "The Workers Party is born out of the workers' desire for political independence. They are tired of serving as electoral fodder for politicians and parties representing the current economic, social, and political order.... Workers want to organize themselves as an autonomous political force." PT also promised it would become a massive party committed to full democracy exercised directly by the masses. The Workers Party's participation in elections and parliamentary activities would serve the objective of organizing the exploited masses and their struggles.

PT became a political home for activists who had survived armed struggle and exile,[1] families of missing political prisoners, and several groups of activists and intellectuals who rejected Stalinism, particularly the methods of the Brazilian Communist Party, and did not desire to compromise with the dictators. Among them were Mário Perdosa, a Trotskyite theoretician and the most eminent art critic in Brazil; Antônio Cândido, a famous literary critic; and Paulo Freire. PT was founded after a series of major strikes that fatally wounded Brazil's military government at the end of the 1970s (Kucinski 2003: 26, 36–37, 39).

In 1978, after rejecting the wage increase offered by the military government, the workers' union leaders were determined to fight for their rights. The first strike broke out in the Saab-Scania truck industry in São Bernardo and later in other multinational companies such as Ford, Mercedes Benz, Volkswagen, and Chrysler. By the end of the second week, approximately eighty thousand workers were on strike. According to Luiz Inacio Lula da Silva (Lula), a unionist and later leader of the Workers Party, it was the first major strike after 1968 supported by workers all over Brazil; furthermore, it was the first time since 1964 that the working class had shown its strength (Branford 2003: 69–70).

At the end of the 1970s, people who had no land, after having claimed and occupied land, started to form themselves into a movement: the "Landless Movement" (MST). This movement, which was supported by PT even though there was no official relationship between the two groups, forced the government to redistribute vast areas of land to three hundred fifty thousand families after long-lasting violent clashes with the police, the army, and privately owned gangs paid by the landowners. Freire's ideas—that people should learn actively, that they should act and speak for themselves, and that what they learn should be based on their own experiences—played an important role in the development of the movement and its pedagogical activities (Wright and Wolford 2003: xiii–xiv, 62, 72–76, 105, 307–315).[2]

The PT was formed by union leaders in a process that, although at first sight looked similar to the one in which European Social Democracy had been created at the beginning of the twentieth century, in fact did not fit any relevant model, not even that of the British Labor Party (PT never had any formal links with the workers' unions, nor was it founded by them). Many Catholics supported PT despite its support of equal rights for homosexuals and legalization of abortion. It attracted a wide range of forces that traditionally were considered incompatible: Trotskyites, Leninists, Marxists, Catholics coming from the liberation theology wing of the church, illiterate workers, and renowned intellectuals.

In a few years, this alliance managed to become the first mass party in Brazil with socialist ideas and members actively involved on a day-to-day basis rather than just during electoral campaigns. It was a mass movement structured like a Leninist party, with a central committee, strict rules about adherence to decisions taken by the party (even though, in actual fact, these were often broken), and allowances for the existence of various tendencies that were systematically organized within the party. Many of its members were also supporters or even leaders of many other social movements that were either not affiliated in any way with PT or, in some cases, even clashed with elected PT local authorities. The most important characteristic of PT as a party was that several different tendencies and schools of thought coexisted under the same roof while respecting the decisions taken by the majority.

Unity in PT was not founded on a vague adherence to or a new particular definition of socialism. It depended fundamentally on an ethos toward society and political involvement that combined radicalism and self-denial. This ethos became the common denominator of all those who participated in the party, irrespective of whether they were intellectuals, workers, Catholics, MST members, or members of women's rights movements. Typical PT members, otherwise known as *petistas*, were radical activists fighting for their rights in movements or communities and not acting out of self-interest.

The main political plan of PT was not the disintegration of the bourgeois state but, instead, the creation of a popular democratic government that would seek viable alternatives to the already existing capitalist social forms. This can be explained by the fact that PT favored an ideological pluralism based on the diversity of its members' social origins (industrial workers, land workers, bank and education employees, smallholders, university professors and students) and also the diversity of their political positions (there were five tendencies of political thought expressed within the party in the mid-1990s) (Kucinski 2003: 26–27, 30–38; Nylen 2000: 140–141; O'Cadiz, Wong, and Torres 1998: 25).

By 1982, PT had two hundred twelve thousand members and, after participating officially for the first time in the elections, won eight seats in the Congress but failed, however, to have a senator elected. In 1986, although its seats in the Congress doubled, the party once again failed to have a senator elected. In 1990, the number of its congressional seats more than doubled (to thirty-five) and a PT senator was elected. No PT candidate managed to get elected as a state governor during that decade. In 1989, Lula, PT's candidate for the presidential elections, won second place, polling 16 percent of the votes; he managed to enter the second round of the elections, where he was defeated after polling 47 percent of the votes as compared to 53 percent polled by Fernando Collor, the subsequent president of Brazil.

Promoting the demand to hold immediate elections and challenging the plan of the military for indirect elections, PT's political campaign, launched in 1984, led the party to success in the 1989 elections. Massive demonstrations and protest marches during this political campaign excited the interest of the entire Brazilian nation. PT was playing a forceful role in the democratization process of Brazil as an established political power fighting its struggles honestly and consistently, without compromise or electoral expediency. PT's performance in the municipal elections took all political analysts by surprise, reversing all the polls. It was quite a remarkable situation for a party that had seen only two mayors elected in 1982 to have this number increase to thirty-two in 1988. One of the cities with a PT-elected mayor was São Paulo, with a population of 10 million inhabitants (Torres 1994a: xi; Nylen 2000: 129–131).

Even if the economic situation of the lower social classes in Brazil worsened at the end of the 1980s, the *petistas* did not win the municipal elections in 1989 for this reason only. The first victories in the 1982 elections had established PT as one of the most influential political forces in local government, with the party's focus on public health, housing, and education. These political priorities proved to be quite successful for PT. For instance, in Diadema, a poor area in São Paulo's industrial zone, PT repeatedly won elections. The idiosyncratic dynamics of the Brazilian political system turned PT into a party that attracted protest votes by offering hope for change to all those in despair (Kucinski 2003: 45).

However, the party was not well prepared to take advantage of its victory or respond successfully to the responsibilities that the local government of big cities entailed in 1988. Apart from PT establishing a reputation for its commitment to democratization, decentralization of local government, and widening of the lower social classes' accessibility to decisionmaking procedures, there was little agreement among *petistas* on PT administration (Baiocchi 2003: 3).

After his return to Brazil, Freire, as already mentioned, joined PT and taught at universities in São Paulo. Luisa Erundina, in her capacity as São Paulo's elected mayor after the PT's victory, offered Freire the post of secretary of education of the municipality of São Paulo, thus giving him the opportunity to be in charge of planning an educational program and to be responsible for educational reform in a city of approximately 10 million people.

As Sampaio regretfully points out, despite the fact that the PT did not take advantage of Freire's affiliation with the Workers Party in order to develop its educational program (cited in Mayo 2004: 101), Freire accepted the offer because it was in alignment with everything he had ever said and done. Otherwise, he would have had to "pull all of [his] books out of press, stop writing, and be silent till death" (Freire 1993b: 58). During his term of office, while meeting with a group of Uruguayan educators, he said: "If I die, for instance, this year, I would not have written the four books I wanted to write, but I proved myself in a job that I needed to perform before dying. Much more necessary than writing those four books was to know how I would behave holding power, and I would like to tell you that I behave well, with a relative coherence" (Schugurensky 1998: 21).

He remained in this post from January 1, 1989, until May 27, 1991, when he resigned to devote himself to writing. The issue of changing curriculum content was quite significant for this reform, which was an undertaking of both practical and theoretical interest. The practical interest consisted of addressing a large population (seven hundred thousand students and thirty-three thousand teachers in six hundred fifty elementary schools); the theoretical interest consisted of Freire, a renowned educator who had never before been involved in curriculum planning for schools in the official school network in Brazil, being responsible for putting such a program into practice.

His appointment to the post of secretary of the municipal educational authorities in São Paulo, the industrial and financial capital of the country, was a major success for the Left in Brazil and symbolized the historical suitability of Freire's thought and confirmed the value of his theoretical principles in educational practice. Freire was considered to be the intellectual and spiritual forefather of those who were at the head of the Workers Party.[3]

In addition to the popularity of his ideas all over the world and their use as a basis for experimentation in some countries,[4] Freire's appointment to such an important post in the official structure of Brazilian education was considered by many Brazilians a milestone in the democratization process of the country. It also boosted the pedagogical passion of all those who were inspired by his thoughts and whipped up an enthusiasm for liberation that characterized the young educators who were born during his exiled years.

The most important goals of this reform were (1) to increase accessibility to education, (2) to democratize educational administration, (3) to improve teaching quality, (4) to provide young workers and adults with educational programs, and (5) to form critical and responsible citizens. To achieve these goals, the municipal educational authorities developed a series of projects that reformed school administration, relations between local communities and schools, and their curriculum. Among the most important projects were the Interdisciplinary Project, planned in order to reform the school curriculum; the Genesis Project, devised for the enhancement of the use of computers; the institutional reorganization of school committees; and the MOVA project, which related to the literacy of youth and adults (O'Cadiz et al. 1998: 71–72; Araujo 1999: 234).

In the nine years that had elapsed since Freire's return to Brazil and before he accepted Erundina's invitation to work as a secretary for the municipal educational authorities, Freire had cooperated with several educators and intellectuals, especially from the United States. His most systematic work was with Henry Giroux, who, according to Oldenski, not only repeatedly acknowledged the relationship between his and Freire's work and their contribution to the development of the discourse of critical pedagogy but also wrote the introduction for two of Freire's books. Conversely, Freire wrote the foreword and the introduction for two of Giroux's books (Oldenski 1997: 71–74). Both educators considered their collaboration to be of substantial importance.

The Brazilian educator also collaborated with several other intellectuals and educators in the writing of books that he called "talking books." Among them were Chilean philosopher Antonio Faundez; U.S. educators Ira Shor, Myles Horton, and Donaldo Macedo; and Mexican professors Miguel Escobar, Alfredo Fernandez, and Gilberto Guevara-Niebla during the 1980s. If we are to understand Freire's political positions before the educational reform that started to take place in São Paulo, we have to focus our attention on this aspect of his writing activity.

After having experienced the disruption of his literacy program by the military coup in Brazil in 1964 and, three years after his departure, the dire end of similar attempts within the framework of agrarian reform in Chile (a result of the military coup of September 11, 1973),[5] the Brazilian educator attempted to produce answers to a series of political questions taking into consideration the controversies entailed in the process of socialist reform in countries that had recently been liberated from colonizers' dominance. These answers relate to undertakings he personally participated in (such as in Guinea-Bissau) in the field of social, political, and ideological struggles. They also relate to a heterodox interpretation of Marxism, which caused his pedagogical thought to thrive and become internationally recognizable.

During the 1980s, this heterodox interpretation of Marxism underwent a crisis. Many academics had already proclaimed that dependence theory seemed to have reached a dead end and was outdated, particularly after the recent democratization of Latin American countries. The Marxist and neo-Marxist versions of this theory were severely criticized for their emphasis on external or international definitions of development and for their insufficient examination of endogenous or domestic ones.[6]

The basic inspiration for this heterodox interpretation of Marxism was the Chinese Cultural Revolution, which had already been quite intensely challenged. After Mao's death in 1975, the subsequent group of leaders rejected the Cultural Revolution and implemented a policy that favored the use of capitalist principles in the economy. In Asia, Africa, and Latin America in some cases, the liberating and revolutionary movements did not manage to overthrow the regimes they revolted against; in some others they ended up being either caricatures of the Soviet regime, asking for its financial and political support (Ethiopia), or theocratic regimes (Iran) adopting a religious fundamentalist perspective. In England and the United States, despite meeting opposition, the neoliberal-neoconservative counterattack was taking shape against the welfare state and the workers' movements under the doctrine "war to the end against the Soviet 'evil empire.'"

There were rays of hope in the increasingly bleak international scene for this specific heterodox interpretation of Marxism. One of these was the Sandinistas' revolution in Nicaragua. Another was the development of social movements after the university students' uprisings in 1968, mainly in countries of the West. As a matter of fact, Nicaragua would become a critical point as well as a point of hope for Freire in the 1980s.

A little while after the revolution in 1979, Freire was invited to help the people of Nicaragua, who had taken history into their own hands. According to Freire, a crucial subject examined during his discussion with Fernando Cardenal, a famous member of the Sandinista government, was how the Miskito natives should be dealt with during the revolution. The Brazilian educator was against imposing a Spanish literacy program on them, a language they did not speak. Their right to use their Creole language, which was based on English, had to be respected by the Sandinistas. In addition, the government of Nicaragua had to guarantee that they would be able to take part in economic and cultural projects.

National unity after the revolution had to be forged on the basis of diversity rather than coercion. Young people who were representatives of the revolution had to be sent to the area where the Miskitos lived to inform them of the literacy project and to clarify that they would not be taught how to read and write in Spanish. Freire was convinced that this position was part of his democratic revolutionary commitment to the reconstruction of society.

According to Freire, unity in diversity is an issue related to the rediscovery of power and struggle. This rediscovery necessarily involves different ways of mass mobilization and organization, different methods, tactics, and strategies; it also shows the undeniable importance of contemporary popular social movements. May 1968 was unequivocally the moment when dissatisfactions emerged. In the 1970s, a great upsurge began of social movements that had been struggling for a long time: women's and gay liberation, ecological as well as racial minority movements that, in actual fact, represented the great majority. Despite the criticism they received, these movements achieved great importance that continued to the end of the century.

After Freire's return to Brazil in 1980, women's struggle against the living conditions they experienced as objects under men's authority was quite impressive. At the same time, a section of the Afro-American population began mobilizing by adopting a different way of reading Brazilian history, giving emphasis to their own contributions to the historical-cultural development of the country, which remained concealed by the officially written history. Women and Afro-Americans, according to Freire, had to struggle by themselves for their own liberation without, however, refusing the help of others. Laborers, for instance, had to accept assistance from intellectuals, because it was both a duty and a right of the latter to participate in the transformation of society. In addition, of particular importance at this period were the struggles of the unions formed by the laborers themselves. The Workers Party was born from all the various activities of the popular movements.

The 1970s were characterized by the growing development of social movements. The revolutionary parties had to work more closely with them in order to prove their authenticity and rethink their own profile; otherwise, they would have been lost in the sense that they would have become more rigid and behaved in an elitist and authoritarian way to the masses whose salvation they claimed to be fighting for. When a nonpopulist party works more closely with certain social movements, then both the party and the movements grow together.

Freire stated that he could not give an answer to those (including himself) who wanted a revolutionary transformation of the bourgeois society into a socialist one—a challenge emerging toward the close of the century. In his opinion, the issue of obtaining power was not as important as that of rediscovering power, which involved a dialectic understanding of the role of the political parties.

Without rediscovering power, people believed that even the mere transformation of society's infrastructure would establish a remarkable perception of power that was mechanistic and illuminated another issue—that of understanding the role of subjectivity in history in its dialectical relationship with objectivity. A critical Left should not be afraid to think about what it would do when in power, even at the most critical moment of the revolutionary transition, that is, when it would have to confront a status quo that was created before the revolution by the bourgeoisie (Freire and Faundez 1992: 62–69; Shor and Freire 1987: 165–166; Giroux and McLaren 1994: 37, 40–41).

Without rejecting his own ideas on the possibility of combining the struggle for independence with the transition toward socialism in countries that had recently won their independence, Freire directed his attention to the more developed countries, relating the level of a country's economic development (reflected in its productivity and technological modernization from a capitalist perspective) to its power to defend itself against economic pressures. Brazil was a useful example. His focus of attention was related not only to his experiences from the previous decade but also to his interest in the social movements and in a corresponding conceptualization of the oppressor-oppressed relationship. According to Freire, there was no universal form of oppression as such; instead, there were a variety of forms of oppression that brought about the development of diverse movements.[7] The term *oppressed* could no longer refer only to the rural masses as he had used it during his years in exile.

By arguing for a variety of forms of oppression, he distanced himself from approaching the oppressed as a class and considered them to be a collection of social groups sharing a common distinctive feature related to oppression (race, gender, social class). These social groups could make up a heterogeneous alliance of forces, their formation based on an essential political position: unity in diversity.[8] Moreover, his cooperation with educators, who during the 1980s attempted to form a critical pedagogy in the United States, seemed to have contributed to turning the position for unity in the context of diversity into an essential element of a policy that corresponded to the needs of a radical, sociopolitical transformation with a socialist orientation in the developed capitalist societies.

For example, in one of the talking books of the 1980s, Freire declared that he totally agreed with Giroux's view relative to the role of social movements in the promotion of democratic principles as agencies of dialogue.[9] The basic problem for educators who dream of change lies in how to perceive this struggle in the sense of generating a new hegemony developed from the manifestations and experiences within these movements (Freire and Macedo 1987: 62).

INTERVENTION IN FORMAL EDUCATION

Drawing from Giroux's analysis of the theories that apprehend education as part of social reproduction, Freire contended that the relationship between education and society was not mechanical but was instead historical, dialectic, and contradictory. From the point of view of the dominant class, the main task of education was to reproduce dominant ideology.

However, dialectically there was also another task—that of denouncing and working against the dominant ideology, a task to be taken over by educators who adopted the political dream of liberation. Someone supporting the status quo could not carry out an educational act that contradicted the reproductionist process. Those who dreamed of rediscovering society had to occupy schools so as to unveil the opaque reality hidden by the dominant ideology, the dominant curriculum.

If from a critical point of view it was impossible to think about education without considering the question of power, if it was impossible to apprehend education as an autonomous or neutral practice, this did not mean that systematic education was equivalent to a pure reproducer of dominant ideology. It is true that education reproduces dominant ideology, but this is not the only thing it can do. The contradictions characterizing society penetrate the educational process and change its role. Reproduction theories tend to fall into a kind of mechanical exaggeration in interpreting the real and concrete fact that the educational system reproduces dominant ideology. The reproduction of the dominant ideology implies an opaque reality, obstructing people from acquiring critical awareness, from critically reading their reality, and from understanding the causes for the facts they have discovered.

In contrast, shedding light on reality is considered to be liberating work within the institutional space of schools. Educators aiming at liberating education should use educational space without being naïve; they should be aware that education is not a lever for revolutionary transformation precisely because this is what education ought to be. This contradiction lies at the heart of the problem. If education were to become a lever for transformation, the social class in power would have to commit suicide and abandon power as well as the supervision of schools. Of course, this has never happened (Shor and Freire 1987: 36–37; Giroux and McLaren 1994: 31; Freire and Macedo 1987: 38–39, 126).

In a discussion with Myles Horton about his experience at the Highlander Folk School, Freire noted that the question about the value of working inside or outside the system refers to the educational system specifically and not the system in general (productive, political, structural), where education constitutes a subsystem. As Kennedy (1981: 105–119) mentions, Horton founded this school in Tennessee in the early part of the 1930s, influenced by the ideas of John Dewey and George Counts and his own experience in similar Danish schools. He aimed at making his school an alternative educational center for those who needed help while conducting social struggles, for those engaged in political rights movements, and for those who were working with the poor. In summary, the school's guidelines were the following: dependence on people's experiences and their need to act upon them; collective self-education, using specialists exclusively as knowledge resources; involvement in new activities that challenged myths and former experiences; use of open and dialogic methods; and a close relationship between analysis and action.

According to Freire, the Highlander school was an example dating back to the 1930s of creating political, cultural, and educational space outside the subsystem of education but also within the system. It would be ideal to struggle against the system fighting on two fronts: inside and outside the school. Outside the school system there would be more space for work, decisions, and choices, but it would also be possible to create space inside the school subsystem. To put it in Freire's words: "That is I think politically, every time we can occupy some position inside of the subsystem, we should do so. But as much as possible, we should try to establish good relationships with the experience of people outside the system in order to help what we are trying to do inside" (Horton and Freire 1990: 202–203).

Before examining the reform in primary schools in São Paulo and the process of planning a new curriculum, I shall refer to the character of the intervention in the official school network proposed by Freire, on the basis of the aforementioned analysis on the relationship between education and the sociopolitical transformation, focusing our attention on his positions on curriculum. To examine the instrumental role of these positions in the formation of his perspective on curriculum planning as expressed in the São Paulo reform, we must take into account how Freire's return to Brazil effected some kind of demystification, as well as consider his involvement in political and pedagogic debates.

According to Tadeu da Silva and McLaren, Vanilda Paiva's critical analysis contributed to the demystification of Freire in his country by associating the birth of his thought with Social Institute of Brazilian Studies reformist ideology. Paiva's work did not, however, suggest any alternative solutions, and the challenge came from a philosopher of education who attempted to build an alternative to Freire's pedagogy. Dermeval Saviani argued that educational practice can be distinguished from political practice even though they are neither independent nor autonomous: every educational practice has a political dimension, just as every political practice has an educational dimension. Education plays a role in the transformation of society, but this role is not directly political. It is political in the sense that education's role is to impart knowledge to the oppressed social classes.

Therefore, Saviani rejected the central idea in Freire's work that education has always been a political activity. He called his perspective historical-critical pedagogy, but in Brazil it was known as the Pedagogy of Contents. Even though Saviani used Antonio Gramsci's work as his main source of reference, he could not ultimately form an alternative pedagogy separated from liberal views on education. He made declarations describing the relations that should exist between education and politics, but he did not analyze the existing ones. He perceived school as a preparatory place for politics in which, however, no policies were carried out and no political debates were conducted. He did not pose any questions on the ways knowledge and science were produced, nor on their relationships to economic production and sociopolitical power. Saviani's interpretation of Gramsci's ideas was similar to Entwistle's (Tadeu da Silva and McLaren 1993: 38–45).[10]

In a letter to North American educators and as part of the publication of a series of educational projects based on his ideas in the United States, Freire expressed his objection to the Pedagogy of Contents; he wrote that progressive educators should never ignore content in order to politicize but, in contrast to reactionists, should always fight to divulge reality to their students, removing anything that hinders them from seeing reality clearly and critically. There was no magical comprehension of content that on its own liberated, nor did the devaluation of the subject matter liberate students as though political perception could by itself be achieved (Freire 1987: 212)

In an interview given after 1992, Freire stated even more clearly his objection to the Pedagogy of Contents, which regarded school as a construction site of knowledge imparted systematically and accurately. To Freire, school continued to be a place of social conflict. In other words, class struggle still took place inside the school. The question was the position of the educator, who should not, of course, stop teaching content in favor of social conflict that emerged both in the world and inside the school. The dichotomy of politics-content was anti-scientific. During the instruction of the appropriate content in the fields of biology, history, or language, it was necessary for class struggle in society to be discussed, clarified, and illuminated (Torres 1998: 98–99).

Freire supported education as an activity of knowledge, a political activity and an artistic event at the same time. He did not talk about a political dimension or a cognitive aspect of education. Education was politics, art, and knowledge (Freire 1985b: 17). As we have seen before, he associated the reproduction of the dominant ideology with its power to blur reality. Consequently, the work of anyone opposing the reproduction of the dominant ideology could only constitute an opposition to the confusion that reproduction caused.

Educators in favor of a liberation process should carry it out through different kinds of educational action: via the instruction of music, mathematics, biology, physics, painting. While the elite was trying to suppress certain issues, liberation educators had to discover ways within the curriculum to analyze these issues. For example, these educators should integrate issues of residential and health care policies in the curricula of architects and nurses by posing questions on the residential and medical needs of people living in slums. This did not, however, require the sacrifice of the curriculum content or the scientific content, nor did it provide a less efficient education.

On the contrary, the inability of a mathematics or a physics teacher to discover relevant issues about his or her subject in various texts, such as World Bank reports, created doubts regarding that teacher's competence. An analysis of the consequences of such texts was associated with scientific problems, thus contributing to the clarification of reality, to the comprehension by students that the process of knowing did not simply mean to devour knowledge but also to comprehend that the latter was a political problem. As much as Freire considered it certain that a biology teacher should teach biology, he considered it equally certain that the phenomenon of life could not be deliberated without discussions of exploitation, domination, freedom, and democracy. The content of a scientific subject could not be separated from its historical and social context. As the teachers should not leave content in parentheses and simply discuss the political situation of the country with their students, they should likewise not put history and social conditions in parentheses, thereby making it clear to their students that there is no such thing as biology per se. Disciplines are not isolated from social life. Teachers should command the content of a curriculum, know how to build it, select and organize it, know how to teach it, be familiar with its history, and by refuting the idea that students are completely ignorant, teachers should consider it their duty to know what their students already know when they come to the classroom (Shor and Freire 1987: 47–48, 69–70, 168; Horton and Freire 1990: 104, 108). As Freire stressed, the educator's task is not to teach students how to think, as they can already do so, but rather to exchange ways of thought and discover together better approaches to decode an object (Frankenstein 1997: 60).

In his discussion with Mexican university professors, Freire dealt with the subject of intervention in the curriculum content in relation to the reproductive role of education, justifying his previous positions with further arguments. Referring to the detachment of the university from the productive process, he stressed that it is possible to ask students to reflect on productive action in the same way that they can be asked to reflect on behavior or political history.

In this way, professors alongside their students could study the reasons that made it fundamental for the bourgeoisie not to reveal the production process, as has been attained in the capitalist economy. At this point, as Freire remarked, he used the conclusions of an article by Braverman in the 1982 *Monthly Review* according to which the more science intervenes or is embodied in the productive process, the less knowledge the working class will have. Agreeing with Braverman, he pointed out that it is a myth to believe that in a developed capitalist economy it is natural that the working social class is more proficient in scientific knowledge because skilled workers are trained in three-hour-long courses to do only the bare minimum on the assembly line.

Based on the foregoing arguments, Freire contended that left-wing intellectuals should know that the level of the less rigorous (precise) knowledge characterizing the working class was not due to a nonexistent ontology. The level or levels of public wisdom could not be explained metaphysically, only historically and socially. Karl Marx knew that within the structures of a capitalist society, the education of workers reproduced them as workers and the education of the bourgeoisie reproduced them as dominators. Consequently, the exact levels of the less rigorous knowledge, formed in a specific manner, should constitute the point where the working class itself aimed at raising its level of knowledge. Freire proposed academic study that had as its starting point the level of the working class and not that of university professors (Giroux and McLaren 1994: 53–55, 143–144, 125–128).

The issue of the content of linguistic instruction was a peculiar case in the wider issue of the curriculum that Freire dealt with in his attempt to formulate an intervention within the context of formal education. As he stressed in his discussion with Shor, language was directly related to the social classes because the identity and power of each social class were expressed in its language, and the forces that ruled society had an extremely elitist norm in terms of which language was judged. This applied particularly to Brazil, where both syntax and ways of thinking were completely different among the various social classes. Educators in favor of an education of liberation should not blame students from lower economic backgrounds for the problems they had with the correct usage of the norm and for the conflict between their language and the dominant forms. Liberation educators had to work with students to help them obtain a solid mastery of the norm and its correct usage, without ceasing the criticism of the political consequences. Students should survive during the struggle for social transformation, despite the danger of assimilating the dominant ideology through the usage of elitist language. Dominant ideology was not reproduced exclusively via language or school. There were other means of social reproduction—language was only one mechanism. Refusing to understand the various forms of language would simply make it more difficult for students to survive during the struggle, whereas what should have been made clear during instruction was that it was essential for them to have control of the norm, not only to survive but also to fight on better terms against the dominant social class (Shor and Freire 1987: 71–73).

These positions on language instruction were typical of the logic whereby the issue of the dominant curriculum had to be approached. By using all dimensions of language, students would become capable of acquiring the curriculum content that corresponded to the interests of those in power. The wealth of scientific study was not something that those in a dependent or oppressed position had no say in because this type of curricular requirement was of interest only to students belonging to the dominant social classes. Students from subordinate social classes needed the skills acquired through the study of the official curriculum, but not at the expense of having a thorough understanding of reality.

Only after these students gained a solid understanding of their world could they attain the selected knowledge contained in the dominant curriculum. This was a goal that could be achieved by students participating in a process of both group and self-empowerment. However, students from subordinate social classes should never allow the knowledge that gave the dominant class an advantage to subdue them or turn them into little oppressors. The dominant curriculum had to be acquired by the dependent students so as to help them in their struggle for social equality and justice (Freire and Macedo 1987: 128).

Studies compel accuracy but not that needed by traditional supporters of the status quo, according to whom reality required only observation rather than interpretation or action. The object of observation did not exist on its own but in the context of a totality. Accuracy would increase provided that observation could go beyond the limits of a simple observation and could become knowledge of the reason for which an object existed. According to Freire, knowing the reason had to do with a historic event, a social activity, not an individual stance. In terms of the curriculum, accurate studies were associated with the study of the classics in all fields with no exclusions.

For instance, students had to study Marxism, positivism, structuralism, and functionalism irrespective of their accepting or rejecting the principles involved. Study was a form of accessing the discourse so that it could be understood from within, as a recognition of the relationship between the text and its context, a discovery of the historic in the text located in the context where it was produced. Criticism of a magical view of the world did not mean the taking of an irresponsible stance in regard to the teachers' and students' obligation to study the classics continually and seriously for a given field of study or to have a command of the texts and to create a respective intellectual discipline.

Pluralism was not an easy project. At university, it did not simply entail different positions but also competitive ones; there were both reactionary and radical professors. The issue, according to Freire, was the discussion of these positions with the students, who had every right to have a reactionary instructor. Many thought that curriculum constitutes a total of subjects, methods, and techniques, whereas in reality it embodied a complete philosophical, political, and epistemological understanding of pedagogy. It was clear that the fight for the curriculum meant pressure on the dominant social classes and the state aiming at the expansion of the space necessary for the struggle. Tolerance, however, was a revolutionary virtue against the danger of the abolition of ideological pluralism, and the dialogue regarding difference was not a sign of bourgeois weakness (Shor and Freire 1987: 83; Giroux and McLaren 1994: 64–65, 91, 96–97, 149; Freire 1991: 143).

CURRICULUM PLANNING AND EDUCATIONAL REFORM

According to the analysis by O'Cadiz et al., as well as other references regarding the educational reform of the São Paulo municipality, when Freire undertook the responsibility for its realization, the main problem he had to face was the miserable condition of public education. Over 1 million children of preschool age as well as children eligible for primary school tuition did not register for school, while the percentage of dropouts and of students judged unfit to continue to the next class was quite high. Thousands of teachers were paid extremely low salaries and worked under insecure terms of employment (temporary employment contracts). Sixty percent of the schools needed immediate repairs: roofs had collapsed, and plumbing and electricity facilities were in serious disrepair. Moreover, the new municipality administration had to face a deficit running in the many millions.

To deal with this situation in primary education, the municipality of São Paulo, with Freire as its head, had three goals: participation, decentralization, and autonomy, all aimed at establishing public education for the masses, which meant that everyone would have access to public education and could participate in building its foundation. Schools would really serve popular interests, the interests of the majority, and would be based on commitment and solidarity, on the formation of class consciousness.

Not only the teachers but also everyone else in school would acquire an active and dynamic role experimenting with new types of learning, participation, teaching, work, play, and festivity. The current practice of parallel school networks in primary and secondary education, meaning a flourishing private sector subsidized by the state, which served the middle class, and, public education for the children of the poor and the working social classes, directly contributed to educational inequality. PT supporters denounced official policies for the privatization of public services and the corrosion in the quality of public schools. As a result, the working class and the peasants faced the dilemma of either being completely excluded from schooling or having to attend a miserable public school.

The concept of public education for the masses was critical to educational reform in São Paulo. Whereas liberal Latin American governments in the nineteenth century had used public education for the masses to define the model of compulsory education as a powerful medium for the promotion of social and national integration of the masses, the new meaning that it acquired was related to the poorer groups of the population becoming involved in individual and collective processes of critical awareness and action. This involvement was associated with issues of access, stability in tuition, and quality of educational opportunities. The goals of public education for the masses entailed increased access to schools, a smooth transition from one level to the next, and a deterrence of students dropping out, as well as an upgrading of structural and organizational functions. Working-class children had to learn to appreciate their own "cultural capital" and participate in learning strategies that would be based on their own "ethos" (in the sense that Bourdieu gave to these two terms).

As Freire wrote, the first step, however, for public education for the masses was the conquest of the old school and its transformation into a research center, a center for pedagogic reflection and experimentation with new alternative solutions from a popular perspective. His proposal was an education of liberation as it espoused conscious, creative reflection and action from the oppressed classes in reference to their liberation process. The people needed a qualitative education in order to obtain hegemony. They needed the tools, the acquisition of knowledge, the methods and techniques, to which only the privileged minority had access. This presupposed the systematic and critical acquisition of reading, writing, and mathematics, as well as of scientific and technological principles. Moreover, it implied familiarity with the methods of knowledge acquisition, production, and transmission: research, discussion, argumentation, use of different modes of expression, communication, and art.

To build this new school, four action areas were defined by the municipality of São Paulo headed by Freire: (1) the democratization of access via the construction of new schools and the expansion-renovation of the existing premises and infrastructure; (2) the promotion of a movement for the education of both the young and adults, with technical and financial support of the social movements already activated in the field of adult literacy; (3) the democratization of the municipal school administration through increased participation and social control, with the creation of institutionalized communication channels and collective decisionmaking methods to activate the preexisting school councils; and (4) the formulation of specific proposals for the improvement of quality in education via the reorganization of school classes into three cycles, as well as the introduction of new evaluation methods, the provision of continuing professional training for teachers, and the establishment of the movement for the reorientation of curriculum through the application of the Interdisciplinary Project and other educational projects (introducing computers in schools, fighting violence, etc.).

The Interdisciplinary Project constituted the driving force of the movement for the reorientation of the curriculum and was founded on the following principles: (a) collective curriculum planning through the process of participation, (b) respect for school autonomy, (c) evaluation of the unity between theory and practice with a methodology of action–reflection–new action, and (d) continuing teacher education on the basis of a developing critical analysis of the curriculum implemented at school. The methodology of curriculum reform started with a process of action–reflection–new action that was developed gradually and collectively by teachers, students, parents, school board members, education specialists from the municipality, schools, and universities with the use of interdisciplinary approaches and the contribution of social movements.

The curriculum reform was divided into three stages: (1) problematization, which included criticism of the existing curriculum and discussion aimed at devising innovative ways to change it; (2) organization, which contained the systematization of the answers in a questionnaire already discussed in schools, as well as the findings of the problematization phase; and (3) planning and implementation of the new interdisciplinary curriculum through the generative theme. The curriculum reform was offered, as a possibility for voluntary reform of the school curriculum, to all interested eight-grade primary schools, and it was based on a well-informed and investigated decision about participation in the project. Those who responded positively (at least 80 percent of the staff) were committed to submitting a proposal with an outline of the expected task. The curriculum reform started with ten pilot schools in 1991 and reached one hundred schools by the end of the mayor's term of office in November 1992.

The generative theme was a road to knowledge of, comprehension of, and intervention in the specific reality under study. It presupposed faith in self-development through collective work, discussion, problematization, formation of questions, conflict, and participation, as well as faith in the acquisition, construction, and reconstruction of knowledge. The generative theme was the interdisciplinary meeting point with all areas of knowledge, and it was based on real-life conditions and problems. The generative themes of public education for the masses were the construction materials for the creation of a curriculum directly associated with local conditions. At the same time, these generative themes correlated the local reality with a wide spectrum of individual, community, and social problems that extended from group relations within the school to public transportation, water, and air pollution in an industrial city such as São Paulo.

The school community, with the assistance of the municipal secretariat, was involved in a preliminary investigation constituting the first phase of curriculum planning. To this end, a variety of methods were employed, including observations; interviews; unofficial discussions with students, parents, and inhabitants; and surveys of the situation in the area, such as demographics, revenue statistics, newspaper articles, and other relevant literature. The goal of this investigation was to distinguish the important situations, that is, the social-cultural-political conditions of everyday life that made up the students' living world.

Teachers became participant observers of the local school reality. They were not to approach the community with a set of preconceptions aimed at confirming their own perceptions; rather, they had to be open, to learn from the community in unexpected ways. Moreover, the community had to be involved both inside and outside the school in a constant process of collective knowledge construction aimed at reacting to the traditional knowledge/power relations reproduced in schools.

Teachers had to select the important situations among the segmental individual experiences of the community, which emphasized individuality, thus offering limited explanations or solutions to the social phenomena they referred to. They selected situations emerging from the discourse of the community and consequently representing a collective dimension, not a strictly individual experience. The important situations could express a specific level of systematization and organization of knowledge for the masses, allowing them to be connected to other views that had not necessarily appeared during the phase of preliminary investigation.

Teachers, focusing on the important situations, worked in groups with the aim of selecting a different theme for each school semester, a theme that would constitute the basis of the curriculum formation. This way, the generative theme, reflecting a fundamental issue or conflict in the school community, became the instrument for the acquisition and construction of knowledge and oriented the whole of the school to the formation of the interdisciplinary curriculum. Even though many generative themes were possible, the team reached an agreement given the particular sociohistorical context of the school and the community as well as current affairs.

In the second phase of curriculum planning, all the subjects to be taught contributed to the learning process through certain themes that referred to the generative theme that had been identified during the investigation of the community's reality. The contribution of the various fields to the study of specific generative themes that oriented the entire work of the school was evidently different from the conventional interdisciplinary approach, which consisted in simply blurring the lines between the disciplines. In contrast, this new approach adopted a critical perspective on the way knowledge was produced in society and how it contributed either to the reproduction of power relations or to the creation of new knowledge and social reform. Despite an effort to remove teachers from the traditional logic of the boundaries of the disciplines, the individuality of each field of knowledge was respected and was used as a point of reference in a continual and collective investigation process regarding a specific theme of sociohistorical importance.

The experts had an important role in the process of planning curriculum and securing a multifaceted approach to reality as a whole. Their continuing effort to allow and promote both school experimentation and the theoretical work done by the scientific personnel of the municipal secretariat resulted in the publication of a series of issues containing the history of certain sciences in the context of Brazilian education (history, geography, mathematics, Portuguese, physics, physical education, arts). Their effort also yielded instructions as to how teachers could integrate the specific content of each subject into the curriculum. Teachers did not have to be isolated in their classrooms; rather, they could work collectively to create the interdisciplinary curriculum, finding ways to thematically combine the content of the different areas of knowledge with their students' sociopolitical reality.

Teachers used the data and the information they had derived from the study of reality to form the generative questions for each of the subjects and the content that had to be taught in each class. In other words, teachers from different disciplines organized their teaching material around a certain generative theme. For each subject, a list of different generative questions was formed. This second phase of the curriculum planning process served to organize the connections between the universe of systematized knowledge and the themes, problems, and important situations that came up during the analysis of the previous phase's findings.

The third and last phase involved the implementation and evaluation of the curriculum, that is, planning activities, which indicated that the students had acquired the knowledge taught. Initially, the teachers decided how they would evaluate this acquisition of knowledge. Group or individual projects were drawn up that allowed students to become actively involved while putting into practice the knowledge they had acquired or constructed. This was a much more authentic and action-directed evaluation strategy than the traditional one. In fact, such types of evaluation techniques presupposed much more time and the use of various means.

Teachers designed situations where student learning corresponded to the three phases of curriculum planning. Initially, students conducted a study in which they collected data that would enable them to comprehend the generative theme and the generative questions (from relative experiences, interviews, observations, written references, archives). Then they organized knowledge by examining the different content areas, and, finally, they applied their acquired knowledge by doing a project that showed their understanding of the different subjects related to the generative theme.

"The evolution of work and its modern aspects" was, for example, the generative theme of one school (Pracinhas da FEB) and was followed by generative questions such as "Is work an instrument to reconstruct society, and does it improve the life of the workers?" Using the generative theme as an umbrella, each teacher developed a group of issues to be investigated. In the history class, students learned about the generative theme by examining the development of labor and workplaces, power relations, historic class struggles, unions, and organized labor. The geography teacher introduced concepts such as land distribution and immigration, as well as the inequalities in the possession of space. The mathematics teacher associated the generative theme with the cost of living, basic calculations, monetary systems, percentages, and fractions. As problems arose, the answers were discovered not only at the intellectual level but also at the activity level. Students, parents, teachers, and administrative staff all took responsibility in the effort for a better future.

The use of only one textbook for the subjects taught and the use of preconstructed teaching plans without the teachers' participation were rejected in favor of a more creative process. Instead, teachers would continually guide research using new and varied sources of knowledge, providing information, and creating learning activities so that students could contribute their own sources of knowledge. The curriculum became a more dynamic, continually developing object of reevaluation and review. The generative theme, rooted in the students' rich culture, was used as the "trunk of the tree of knowledge," which grew based on the initial investigation of the community's reality. Its "branches" extended to the different knowledge areas in search of the necessary connections in order to attain a better understanding of the reality from which they were separated.

According to an evaluation of the results of the four-year-long educational reform in São Paulo, there was an increase of 15.59 percent (120,358 students) in the number of public school students compared to 1988. It is estimated that 45,000 students did not lose a year. Student failure was drastically reduced, especially in the first and fifth grades, where the percentage was traditionally high. The school failure percentage in São Paulo was reduced to 22 percent, even as the mean failure in Brazil reached 50 percent. The percentage of school dropouts in 1992 was 5 percent, one of the lowest rates in the world.

Reactions to the reform were varied. As far as teachers were concerned, their reactions ranged from acceptance and support, particularly by those who had previously experienced the poverty of their students, to suspicion and resistance by those who did not support PT and looked upon the generative theme as a vehicle for the promotion of party propaganda because the generative themes focused on social issues. Some misinterpreted the curriculum philosophy and acclaimed it for the wrong reasons, others followed it because of the extra payment provided but did not change their teaching methods, and still others complained about the increased work they were required to do. Despite the efforts of the municipal secretariat in the direction of a nonselective education, some teachers were biased toward certain students in their classrooms.[11]

Even though the reform was associated with social movements and many teachers were impressively successful in the implementation of the Interdisciplinary Project, others faced serious problems, mainly because the issue of gender was not thoroughly examined and there was no subsequent support. As a result, a significant opportunity to reinforce the realization of the overall goals of the project was lost. There were reactions to the reform from the bureaucratic mechanisms, which Freire called threatening and irrational. But he never defined the origin of these reactions or the interests that had been damaged. Moreover, there was tension between PT leaders' positions about the state and the pursuit of autonomy by the social movements.

Freire criticized a number of the basist leaders, who excessively projected its values, that is, that knowledge and wisdom were found in the masses and that those who disagreed were either elitists or academics. He considered their perspective to be the foundation of an anti-intellectual approach to education and politics. This kind of criticism revealed the conflict in the way the municipality administration approached education and the way social movements with a basist political philosophy did. At the same time, there were conflicts between the party and the municipality administration. PT leadership in São Paulo, for example, accused Mayor Erundina and Freire of a fascist exercise of power; there were also, of course, attacks by conservative academics and reporters. The party leadership, nominee President Lula, and Mayor Erundina supported Freire against these attacks (O'Cadiz et al. 1998: 4, 7–8, 22, 26–29, 43, 48–52,

73, 85–90, 93–94, 109–133; Saul 1993: 145–165; Wong 1995: 128–129; Torres 1994b: 195–211; Gadotti 1994: 101; Sieber 1997: 280; Rossato 2002: 159; Mayo 2004: 29).

During his service as secretary of education in the municipality of São Paulo, Freire gave a series of interviews that were published in 1993 in a book titled *Pedagogy of the City*. In it he argued that the process of reforming the curriculum could not be constructed in every detail by a group of experts who would devise prepackaged curricula to be executed according to thoroughly prepared instructions and guidelines.

Curriculum reform had always been a political-pedagogical process, which had to be substantively democratic. Each pedagogic plan was necessarily political and filled with ideology. The issue was fundamentally political because it was impossible to have an educational practice devoid of content, devoid of an object that would be taught by an educator and would constitute an object of knowledge for students. The issue had to do with which content to teach and to whom, for what reason, and for whom and against whom; how it should be taught; and how students, parents, teachers, and grassroots movements would participate in discussions about the organization of the content. In the interviews included in *Pedagogy of the City,* Freire supported positions similar to the ones he had supported in the 1980s before undertaking the responsibility of reform. These positions were put into practice via the official curriculum reform process in the municipality of São Paulo.

As for defining curriculum content, he stressed that educators should not ignore knowledge coming from the students' lived experiences, which they brought to school. On the contrary, through those experiences educators should lead students to more rigorous knowledge. Children from the lower social classes had the right, proportionate to their age, to be informed about and shaped according to the advances of science, but the school system had to understand and value the knowledge of their social class because all this knowledge had been socially and historically produced and there was no knowledge that could be presented as unsurpassable.

The educational work initiated from the students' worldview was undoubtedly one of the fundamental elements upon which educational practices had to be built. Student participation should not be understood in simplified terms. Freire proposed a pedagogy that would start from the knowledge brought to school by students (this knowledge was an expression of their social class), a pedagogy that would surpass this knowledge, but not in the sense of subverting it or of imposing other knowledge on it. Respect for cultural identity and rejection of linguistic discrimination that derives from class and racial prejudice are two characteristic positions of his on the question of language teaching. He rejected not only the elitist approach that the language of the lower social classes was inferior and repulsive but also the sectarianism that characterizes the rejection of the idea that the subordinate classes need to master the dominant language so as to survive and fight for the transformation of society.

As far as the content of knowledge is concerned, he would use the difference between the practices of a progressive educator and those of a conservative educator in order to reiterate the substance of a position that he had held in the 1980s. For both the progressive and the conservative educator, four times four equals sixteen, but for the progressive content instruction always had to be linked with a critical reading of reality and with teaching how to think and study, how to approach the objects to be taught, how to apprehend the importance of research about knowledge. Content could not be taught as if the school context could be reduced to a neutral place where there were no social conflicts and where the content could be disconnected from the exercise of thinking correctly. Teaching content based on a progressive educational practice entailed unveiling the causes of the problems, provoking students to understand that the world that is presented as a given is actually made and, precisely for this reason, that it can be changed, transformed, and reinvented (Freire 1993a: 23–24, 40–41, 77, 112–113, 134–135).

In a discussion with Moacir Gadotti, Freire, after he had resigned from the secretariat and after conservative political forces had regained the municipality of São Paulo,[12] stated that he did not feel sorry for his choices in favor of autonomy and popular participation, in favor of an open, joyful, creative, democratic public school for the masses, a school that, even though it had the people's *"taste and smell,"* was not repugnant to the children of the bourgeoisie. Despite the loss of the administration of the São Paulo municipality, it was nonetheless possible to continue the struggle for the implementation of education for the masses, albeit under unfavorable terms.[13] An aspect of this struggle would have to be the educator's attempt to comprehend culture from a multicultural perspective, with the involvement of the students commenting on the differences and showing that this part of the curriculum was not universal. There were peripheral and family dimensions in the curriculum, and they were connected to the problem of social classes (Freire and Gadotti 1995: 264–270).

THE FINAL TEXTS

Freire's basic political ideas, supported in the 1980s, did not change radically in his texts written in the 1990s, that is, after his resignation from the post of the secretary of education in the municipality of São Paulo. One of the reasons for some modifications may be found in the fall of the so-called existing socialist regimes.

As the analysis of Freire's political positions shows, he had never been an advocate of the Eastern European regimes. In his texts there were only indirect critical references to their character, even though the theoretical and political positions in these texts were clearly dissociated from the orthodox interpretation of Marxism and the political agenda of the communist parties affiliated with the Soviet Union. Irrespective of the interpretations that can be made about his political stance before the fall of the regimes of Eastern Europe, the actual fact is that this changed after 1991.

Freire argued that the failure of "existing socialism" did not come about because of the socialist dream but because of the authoritarianism that characterized it and was in contrast to this dream. Joseph Stalin was not the only person to blame for this authoritarianism; Karl Marx and V. I. Lenin were equally accountable because they did not value the positive element of democracy in the capitalist experience. Thus, Freire referred to an authoritarian socialism also characterized by dogmatism, lack of flexibility or deproblematization of the future, brutality, sectarian blindness, and an inclination to bureaucratic immobility. He also talked elsewhere about mental bureaucratization, the reduction of life to immobility, a mechanistic comprehension of history that nullified freedom, choice, decision, and conviction.

This did not mean that Freire denied the fundamental reasons for the disintegration of the regimes, which in his opinion were materialistic, economic, and technological. The fall of the regimes, however, offered the obscure and tempting challenge to continue the struggle for the socialist dream cleansed of authoritarian deformations, vulgar absolutisms, and sectarian blindness. The fall of the Eastern European regimes did not signal the end of history (Freire 1999b: 96, 115–116; Freire 1996a: 84, 165; Freire 1998b: 48–49; Freire and Macedo 1995: 391).

Nevertheless, this criticism did not lead Freire to fully reject Marx's work. During his service as secretary of education in São Paulo, he stated that, although he had never been among those who deified Marx, this did not mean he agreed with those who claimed that Marx no longer had something to say. There was a big difference between recognizing the complexity of certain societies with a high level of capitalist development, a complexity that required a fine adaptation of the Marxist tools of analysis used to understand these societies better, and denying the existence of social classes, with their contradictory interests (Freire 1993b: 134).

Not only did Freire try to explain his political positions on the fall of the Eastern European regimes, but he also attempted to clarify his position on class struggle, which had been a hot issue for the critics of his work, including his positions on two closely related issues: the role of the social movements and the concept of unity in diversity. Thus, he stressed that he had never worked under the false conception that social classes and the struggle between them could explain everything (neither could gender or race do so) and that he had never written that class struggle in the modern world was the driving force of history. Nevertheless, it was impossible for someone to understand history without taking into account the social classes and their conflict of interests. Although class struggle was not *the* driving force of history, it was certainly one of them.

Intercultural differences existed in various dimensions (class, race, gender, and, ultimately, ethnicity). They created ideologies that were ideologies of discrimination *and* ideologies of resistance. Unity in diversity constituted the only effective response of those who, according to the ancient rule of the powerful, the rule of division and submission, were forbidden to exist. Not much had changed between 1973, when he had first expressed the proposal for unity in diversity at a conference in Chicago, and 1994, when, during a reevaluation of *Pedagogy of the Oppressed,* he realized that serious antiracist and antisexist movements systematically refused to include the concept of class struggle in a comprehensive analysis of racism and sexism and the struggle against them.[14]

Unity refers not to antagonistically different groups but to different groups that are reconcilable. The former, within the process of the struggle, might reach an agreement as a result of circumstantial objectives that serve both extremes, whereas among the latter unity would be founded on strategic and not merely tactical objectives. The struggle of women, men, blacks, workers, Brazilians, and Americans was influenced by gender, race, social class, culture, and history.

Starting from this definition, however, the fight had to converge in the direction of humans being more "human." The gradual overcoming of every kind of discrimination was part of the liberation dream, of the quest for happiness, of life itself. Unity within diversity did not entail uprooting or underestimating difference in order to create a totality; nor did it entail homogenization. Rather, unity in diversity entailed a common struggle against inequality, a common struggle of oppressed groups for freedom. One of the fundamental problems in tactics was how the oppressed would understand their position and unite their powers to effectively and successfully confront their biggest enemy (Freire 1999b: 90, 150–159, 187; Freire 1998c: 35–36, 85; Freire 1998b: 85–87; Freire 1996a: 160–165, 177; Leistyna 2004; Freire and Macedo 1993: 174).

Because he did not believe that Stalinist authoritarianism was inherent in socialism, nor did he accept that there was an onto- logical incompatibility between human beings and the essence of socialism (on the contrary, what human ontology rejected was authoritarianism, irrespective of its definitions), there was no reason he should not accept that democratic socialism was a proposal that could be implemented. Progressive parties would either be re-created and discover themselves in the radicalness of their dreams, or they could decay in their devotion to muti- lating sectarianisms, suffocating due to Stalinist ideology. Some ex-progressive and current realists, when they claimed that the fight had to be given for democracy, continued to juxtapose socialism to it, thus repeating the old mistake that democracy was the exclusive property of the bourgeoisie. If the dream of the rising bourgeoisie was capitalism as the seal of bourgeois democracy, the dream of the masses had to be socialism as the seal of popular democracy. The fundamental issue was not the denial of democracy but its perfection. Socialism had to be its content. Capitalism could not be made more humane—that was a dream that could not be realized and a dream that only angels or unreformed deceivers could be devoted to (Freire 1998b: 49; Freire 1998a: 14, 59; Freire 1996a: 114, 137, 188).

In the texts written after 1992, Freire supported similar positions to those of the 1980s, on which the curriculum plan- ning of the São Paulo reform was based, regarding the issue of intervention in the formal school network. The content of the subjects should not be separated from their social context, nor should it be dissociated from critical discussion related to the social, political, economic, and cultural reality, or dissociated from other forms of knowledge and values that rarely constituted part of the curriculum. The children of the masses, of the people, had to learn the same mathematics, the same physics, and the same biology as the children coming from the "more prosperous areas" of the city, but, at the same time, the progressive educator should never accept that the teaching of any subject could avoid a critical analysis of the operation of society (Freire 1999b: 78, 111; Freire 1998a: 36, 47–48, 58; Freire 1998c: 58, 65–66; Freire 1998b: 44–45, 75; Freire 1996a: 118, 155; Freire 2004: 19–20).

Education for the masses, irrespective of where and when it was implemented, could not be detached from involving the students and educators with the causes of the events. A progressive understanding of education should not be reduced to technical and professional training necessary for the workers; a training that simply reproduced people within a social class in the context of neoliberal realism, promoting their adaptation to the world rather than transforming the world. It should not dissociate technical skillfulness from the philosophical ability to think, practical ability from intellectual exercise, theory from practice, and economic from political production (Freire 1999a: 102, 131; Freire 1998a: 126–127; Freire 1996a: 131; Rossato 2005: 16; Freire 2004: 36).

Support for the social and cultural empirical knowledge of students had to constitute the point of departure for the definition of curriculum content, and this did not mean an indefinite rotation around this knowledge, or mystification, but, rather, respect of the knowledge of the masses and the corresponding cultural context, as well as a widening of the horizons of necessary scientific knowledge.[15] Pedagogic difficulties would have been reduced had schools taken into consideration culture, language, an effective way of learning mathematics, and knowledge of the world of the oppressed in order to process the content and its organization in the curriculum so that students could move on to more rigorous knowledge (Freire 1999b: 69–71, 84–85; Freire 1998b: 72, 74, 83; Freire 1996a: 16).

Language based on concepts that developed within the framework of everyday life and language based on abstract concepts were equally rich and beautiful. It was necessary for children of the subordinate classes to learn the dominant code so as to reduce the disadvantages they faced and to earn a fundamental tool in their fight against injustice and discrimination (Freire 1995: 63; Freire 1998b: 22, 74). Progressive educators should not limit themselves to presenting their own reading of the world, which they were anyway obliged to do, because the opposite constituted a hypocritical acceptance of a nonexistent neutrality in education (pedagogic practice always has a direction).

They had to admit that there were other readings of the world, different and at times antagonistic to their own. This, of course, presupposed integrity and knowledge of the various views that had nothing to do with the imposition of their own opinions. On the contrary, one of the forms of imposition was the so-called objectivity and nondirectionality, because not creating pedagogical structures where the educator could make it possible for the oppressed to regain what they were denied (among which were their ability to think critically and their choice to act as subjects of history) constituted a covert imposition of the oppressive conditions responsible for their submission (Freire 1999b: 112; Freire 1995: 65; Freire 1998a: 24, 68; Freire and Macedo 1995: 378, 388–390).

4

CONCLUSIONS

~⊖~

THE FORMATION AND CHARACTER
OF FREIRE'S PERSPECTIVE

Since his childhood, Freire had been acquainted with the values of Catholicism, with a middle-class ethos of dialogue and respect, but also with the very difficult living conditions of the working class and lower strata of northeastern Brazil. The underdevelopment of this area and the economic crisis at the end of the 1920s had a direct impact on his living conditions and education, as well as constituting the primary factors in the development of his ideology and political persona. Christian humanism, in the sense that progressive Catholic intellectuals attributed to it, was a basic ideological direction that determined his thought.

During his employment at the Social Service of Industry, the ideas of the New School (an international movement that had influenced the discussion on education and educational theory in Brazil since the beginning of the twentieth century) that he had primarily adopted were put to the test when he was called on to meet the educational needs of the workers. Even though the foundation and operation of this service aimed at the reinforcement of the bourgeois sociopolitical regime's ideology, Freire tried to utilize its contradictions and contribute to its democratization. This undertaking failed, and he attributed its failure to the paternalistic character of the whole attempt—it ignored the needs of and issues of concern to the workers themselves.

Through this failure he came to realize that the use of the ideas of the New School did not suffice to create a different prospect for the education of the working class, which lived in hideous conditions. His combined employment for almost twenty years at the Social Service of Industry, the Movement for Popular Culture, and the University of Recife focused on these lower social classes that, from the mid-1950s until the coup in 1964, gradually became more radical.

The radicalization of the working classes was due to the aggravation of social problems and the fact that the Brazilian political leadership of the 1950s was not solving them. Radicalization was expressed through changes in the correlation of power in the trade unions, the formation and expansion of the peasants unions and the rural leagues, the fragmentation of the youth of Catholic Action, and the formation of Popular Action and the Movement for the Education of the Base. In the political arena, the formation of popular political fronts in northeastern Brazil and the shift toward the left, promoted in an ambivalent manner by the political forces that supported the Joao Goulart's presidency in the early 1960s, sustained each other through radicalization. One of the basic elements of these developments was the emergence of literacy as an issue of primary political importance.

The radicalization of the lower social classes influenced the thought of the intelligentsia and vice versa. The Social Institute of Brazilian Studies, the main pole of attraction for Brazilian progressive intellectuals of the period, formulated a vision of a self-reliant national development that combined mainly two ideological elements: nationalism and an emphasis on development. Freire was fascinated by that vision and believed that it could be realized, with maximum possible consistency, within the framework of the specific transitional period that Brazil was then undergoing.

According to the historical analysis of the Brazilian educator, dependence, a residue of the colonial past, constituted a central

Conclusions

sociopolitical problem. The process of urbanization continued to bear the mark of the ambiguous interactions of a national-democratic type of political structure based on a feudal economic and social infrastructure. What was required was the completion of the industrialization and urbanization already in progress, as well as the formation of a new relationship between the socioeconomic structure and the political superstructure. Such a relationship would take into consideration the new data, would serve the needs of the country, and would be characterized by the active participation of the popular masses.

This last point is crucial. Freire's focus on the working classes' active participation was founded on his faith in humanization, which portrayed people as creators of history and culture; on his rejection of the existence of absolute ignorance; on his reservations about the consequences of the modernization of technology and production; and on his immediate and personal involvement in one of the many forms of radicalization of the masses: the Movement for Popular Culture, through which experts did not work "on" or "for" but *with* the working class.

A militant democracy, that is, a democracy that did not serve the purpose of the legalization of sovereign power and was not restricted to political governance, but rather constituted a way of life, had to be the basic characteristic of self-reliant socioeconomic development in Brazil. It constituted a form of democracy that did not exceed the boundaries of the bourgeoisie. By the time of the military coup in 1964, Freire had evolved into a radical liberal-Christian humanist educator.

Militant democracy constituted the central political goal of Freire's literacy program within the framework of the Movement for Popular Culture and was standardized in the city of Angicos. It was a political goal similar to the one adopted by John Dewey, one of the most prominent U.S. founders of the New School movement. However, the democracy that the Brazilian educator supported was characterized by radical arguments that arose during the process of his personal ideological and political development.

The political goal of the literacy program ambiguously included the liberal legacy of the New School expressed by the strengthening and deepening of democracy within the bourgeois regime and the active participation of the masses. In order for the central political goal to be realized, the educational process (in this case a semiformal literacy process that was not included in the official educational system but was supported by the government) had to aim at critical consciousness. The latter was the result of a three-stage process during which the transition from the first stage to the second (semi-intransitive and naïve transitive consciousness, respectively) was almost automatic, triggered by wider sociopolitical changes. The intervention of education was necessary for there to be a transition from the second to the third stage, critical consciousness.

Freire's scheme of conscientization took the direction of elevating consciousness to the level of understanding the causes of the physical and social phenomena, based on mechanistic logic. The change of consciousness was not related to social and political juxtapositions but was presented as the ultimate result of either socioeconomic modernization or the influence of education. This change was thus presented as being disengaged from the problem of the radical transformation of the social and political relationships and practices as a whole. In this sense, the liberal legacy of the New School was also present in the educational goal of the literacy program.

However, the starting point for defining the content included in the planning of the literacy program, that is, the dependence on students' basic concepts, ideas, and practices that offered possibilities for discussion about everyday life within a social, political, and cultural framework, was in contradiction to the mechanistic understanding of the process of conscientization. It corresponded to the radical aspect of the program's political goal, that is, the active participation of the working classes in the formation of the social and political life of the country. Research on the vocabulary used by those the program was called on to address was based on Freire's belief that change in Brazil had to be founded on the culture of these classes and their knowledge of the world. The program's planning process was not to be conducted solely by associates (such as researchers and teachers) and experts, without the people it was meant to address.

More contradictions in the planning of the literacy program can also be detected in the emphasis on teaching the ten sketches that referred to the culture-nature distinction before teaching generative words as an introductory phase to the main part of the program. The influence of the liberal pedagogy of the New School, which based the program on the way that the experts and their associates understood the needs of the students, was evident here as well and contradicted the construction of codifications based on the research of the participants' vocabulary.

Although the literacy program was in part based on those student concepts, ideas, and practices that offered possibilities for discussion on everyday life in a social, political, and cultural framework, and in part on how the experts and their associates understood social reality, the content of teaching was selected and organized without the participation of the students. This meant that the students did not become co-researchers; nor was the totality of the program's content based on the students' input. The important role of the experts was also evident in the way the literacy program intended to influence education in Brazil through its extension to a postliteracy program. The experts determined to a large degree not only the organization of the main content that was to be taught in teaching units, but also its enrichment. Along with the experts and the social and natural reality, the students, being the ones who determined the issues included in the program, were also involved.

Given the aforementioned ambiguities, Freire's literacy program prior to 1964, even though it entailed a different starting point for the definition of content selection, did not represent a perspective for curriculum planning different from those that appeared in the United States. Because of these ambiguities, the literacy program can be characterized as a hybrid, with a predominantly liberal perspective, because its set goals (similar to those of Dewey) were, after all, sustained by the other elements of curriculum planning.

The Brazilian educator had formulated a radical liberal proposition for curriculum planning, a radical version of the liberal perspective that Dewey had expressed at the beginning of the twentieth century. This explains why James Howe, director of the United States Agency for International Development, declared that the Freire "method" was not one of Marxist indoctrination. However, what Howe could not foresee or accept was that the content of Freire's program in that particular conjuncture of mobility and radicalization of the masses "seemed to be adequate both for the use of populist politicians and the more leftist popular northeastern fronts. At the end of Goulart's regime, using this method meant defending national reforms against imperialism. The method's objective was the 'democratization' of Brazil and this could be interpreted in many ways" (Facundo 1984: 4–5).

In other words, Freire's literacy program planning could implicitly and conditionally be utilized within the context of different sociopolitical strategies. The main reason was that it was based, even though not exclusively but quite significantly, on an investigation of students' concepts, ideas, and practices, which offered opportunities for discussion on everyday life within a social, political and cultural framework. This pivotal point for the definition of curriculum content imparted a potential popular-democratic character to the program and provided the opportunity for it to be used in a context different from that of liberalism. The military coup of April 1, 1964, did not, however, enable the verification of this potential.

After the failed attempt to open a new political path in Brazil and the tragic consequences of the military dictatorship, Freire distanced himself from populist leaders, seeking a new political orientation. The Chile of the second half of the 1960s became Freire's laboratory for ideological and political exploration. The basic ideological-political preconditions for the writing of *Pedagogy of the Oppressed* included the aggravation of class conflicts in Chile; the fact that the practices used by the Christian Democrat government for rural reform were challenged by the social and political forces of the lower classes, in combination with the emergence of the liberation theology movement; the attraction of the practices of the revolutionary leadership in Cuba; and the Cultural Revolution in China (these last two events were matters of concern not only for the intellectuals in Santiago but also for intellectuals worldwide). With *Pedagogy of the Oppressed,* Freire made a huge political leap compared to his work before 1964. Despite his initial position, which supported a militant democracy that did not exceed the boundaries of the bourgeois regime, he now favored a radical sociopolitical transformation with a socialist orientation. He did not believe, however, that this transformation had to be theoretically separated and realized in two stages (bourgeois-democratic and socialist) as the strategy of the orthodox communist parties (those who supported the official policy of the Soviet Union leadership) dictated.

As far as the Brazilian educator was concerned, the subject of radical transformation was not primarily the working class but the oppressed or "the people," which included workers and farmers as well as any other oppressed social stratum or group. This approach was founded on a vague interpretation, different from the typical Leninist definition of social class (based on the concept of exploitation), that resulted in an inadequate analysis of social structure. However, this view signaled Freire's shift to the left.

Criticism of the Soviet Union and the way that orthodox communist parties were organized and operated was at the core of Freire's political positions regarding the relationship between the revolutionary leadership and the people. The revolution had to be continual, and its central focus both before and after coming to power should be to promote dialogue between the leaders and the people. It should not be conducted in the *name* of the people but *with* the people. It had to be a revolution where, after coming into power, education would be the determinant both of its success and of its nonbureaucratic nature, so that, as Freire (indirectly but at the same time quite explicitly) suggested, what happened in the Soviet Union could be avoided.

Without a cultural revolution as a process that would transform people's consciousness, the structural transformations were at risk of losing their meaning and being fossilized. A relationship between leadership and the people that was founded on dialogue would form the core of a different perspective for the role of vanguard as opposed to the one determined by the leaderships of the orthodox communist parties of the period. The logic of the vanguard party, which had the monopoly of knowledge and revolutionary consciousness, was a basic element of Freire's critique. On this criticism he based his position about the necessity of a leadership that had to be founded on the people's empirical knowledge, which this leadership would enrich with its own knowledge in order to be gradually converted into knowledge on the causes of reality (by the leadership and the people) through dialogue.

Moreover, his critical observations about the dangers of consumerism and bureaucracy in postrevolutionary Guinea-Bissau were related to his views on a balanced economic development of the primary and secondary sectors of production as well as the orientation of production toward values of use. All these critical observations and positions constitute his critique of the regimes of Eastern Europe and imply his positive attitude toward the so-called Chinese way to socialism. The Cultural Revolution was a source of inspiration for the Brazilian educator.

Besides, Freire's respect for Mao Zedong's policy was stated in a very direct way. According to Freire, V. I. Lenin, Fidel Castro, and Mao were the leaders who attempted to respond to the problem of the obstinacy of the old way of thinking after the Russian, Cuban, and Chinese revolutions, respectively. Mao, by means of the Cultural Revolution, had provided the best answer of the century (Freire 1973: 26).

Another source of inspiration was dependence theory. Even though by adopting its fundamental positions, Freire overcame the idea that dependence was a vestige of the colonial past of the pre-1964 period, he nevertheless underestimated the needs of the specific historic, social, and political analysis of the social formations he referred to. As Milios notes, theories of dependence ascribe priority to the world economy and global economic and social relationships over the economic processes and particular social relationships that condition national social formations (Milios 1997: 50–65). Global practices are supposed to govern the procedures in the interior of every social formation as well as determine their evolution; this results in dependence being the most essential feature of the social relations of countries of the periphery. Along with Freire's lack of substantial sociopolitical analysis, we have to consider his lack of a broad and systematic analysis of the dominant culture highlighted by Mayo (1996: 155). These specific shortcomings contributed to Freire's reduction of the complex sociopolitical confrontations into a binary opposition of oppressors/oppressed. In a period when the working class of the metropolitan capitalist states of the West seemed to slow down the revolutionary pace, the challenge to imperialism and the opening of the path for radical sociopolitical transformation would have to be taken up by the fronts of the oppressed social classes, strata, and groups in countries of the periphery.

The peasants seemed to have greater revolutionary potential than the working class in the countries referred to in Freire's educational theory. The revolutionary process would have to be uniform, without distinct stages, because the revolutionary leaderships could not wait for the sociopolitical and ideological strengthening of the working class in their countries but had to rely on those fronts whose main force were the peasants following the examples of China, Cuba, and Vietnam.

Freire's positions were along the lines of a heterodox interpretation of Marxism advanced by intellectuals in the West (which was presented in Chapter 2 and based on Coletti's analysis): a questioning of the political strategy of the two stages; a different approach to the subject of sociopolitical transformation; the fundamental significance of the educational factor in the revolutionary process; criticism of bureaucratization and of bourgeois logic and practices in the transition to socialism; a challenge to the notion that knowledge was an exclusive possession of the revolutionary vanguard; and adoption of basic principles of dependency theory. At this juncture, Freire cannot be considered a Marxist, because the influence on him of other schools of thought, such as phenomenology, existentialism, and Hegelianism, cannot be underestimated. He can, however, be characterized as a *Marxisante*, a term that in Brazilian means "not completely Marxist but someone who is inspired by and friendly to Marxist revolutionary ideas" (Coben 1998: 71). Therefore, Freire's political leap, in the light of the sociopolitical events and ideological conflicts that convulsed the world at the end of the 1960s, as well as the disillusionment in the democratic and liberal route toward national development in his country due to the military coup, was in the direction of a heterodox, rather than the dominant, interpretation of Marxism. In *Pedagogy in Process*, Freire significantly closed the gap in his definition of the radical sociopolitical transformation that had been evident in *Pedagogy of the Oppressed*. Having this small African country as his theoretical and practical benchmark, Freire not only attempted to actively contribute to its reconstruction and orientation toward a socialist perspective but also tried to form a cognate framework of political theses on the relationship between education and sociopolitical transformation through the linkage of education and production.

According to Freire, education had to be directly connected to production but not with the exclusive goal of increasing production through the provision of technical and scientific knowledge. Labor played a key role in social organization and constituted the main source of knowledge. Increase in production could not be achieved without the political conscientization of the masses, without the development of solidarity, social responsibility, and camaraderie. Moreover, within the framework of social transition, scientific and technical education could not be disengaged from the comprehension of the production processes that would put people in charge of them. Socialism was not simply capitalism without capitalists but a society in the process of a cultural revolution.

The publication of *Pedagogy in Process* ends the second period of the Brazilian educator's work. However, adopting this specific heterodox Marxist interpretation does not mean that Freire abandoned Catholicism. In the years of exile, he presented a radical interpretation of Christianity;[1] his ideas had already influenced liberation theology. He wrote: "I went to the slums of Brazil not because of Marx but because of Christ. The people in the slums told me: 'Go, meet Marx.' Their conditions sent me to Marx. Now I meet both, Marx and Christ, and I have no problems" (quoted in Mathew 1980: i). This contradictory coexistence of different philosophical approaches in his work should not give rise to any questions. The Brazilian educator never, in any of the periods of his work, proposed a theory free of contradictions, nor did he ever claim to have done so.

Despite the syncretism characterizing his work, adopting a heterodox Marxist interpretation during his years in exile entailed the espousal of a radical sociopolitical transformation, with a socialist orientation, as the main political goal of the curriculum planning. It further entailed the projection of critical consciousness as the end result of the conscientization process, which changes meaning when placed in the context of the struggles of the oppressed against their oppressors.

This radical sociopolitical transformation and an attempt to form a revolutionary pedagogy gave conscientization new content. Conscientization was conceived both as an approach to a particular worldview founded on the collective criticism of lived experiences and as an act of liberation in attempting to overcome these experiences. This is a radical change when compared to the goals of the literacy program before 1964, a change that constitutes the foundation of Freire's perspective on curriculum planning.

As far as the departure point for the selection of curriculum content is concerned, it relied on the people's beliefs about social reality and on their perception of the world. The projection of this view in *Pedagogy of the Oppressed* was purely political. The most important difference in curriculum planning that Freire proposed in this classic volume was that he no longer supported the instruction of preselected content as he had in his pre-1964 literacy program. The instruction of the ten sketches, which helped learners distinguish nature from culture in the introductory stage of that program, was directly influenced by the liberal education of the New School movement.

The discussion of generative themes could lead to many other issues and thus serve as a rationale for teaching that Freire called "problem posing," which he considered different from problem solving.[2] In addition, generative themes were connected to limiting situations, a key concept for understanding the themes' relationship to the new meaning of conscientization, because this connection did not separate reflection from the practice whose goal was radical sociopolitical transformation.

Praxis (unity of theory and practice) was one thesis about the definition of curriculum content. Another was that of relating content to social context by including the contradictions characterizing the region where the program would be implemented in the content of the curriculum. These two theses (praxis and relevance to the social context) constituted the starting point of Freire's reliance on the people's beliefs about social reality and were fundamental for the selection of curriculum content.

These positions as a whole, during the years in exile, constitute a perspective of curriculum planning that overcomes the contradictions between the liberal and the radical elements contained in Freire's theses on the planning of the literacy program before 1964. It is a qualitative modification based initially on Freire's change in political orientation. In the pre-1964 period, Freire did not accept that associates (researchers and educators) and experts had unlimited power, because the literacy program then was partially founded on the generative words of the participants, who did not actually participate in the research process. At the end of the 1960s, Freire espoused a collective curriculum planning process involving associates, experts, and participants residing in the area where the program was to be implemented. The participants were involved in each and every planning stage of the literacy program. This involvement, however, did not imply equal roles for associates, experts, and participants; this was the case for three reasons. First, the participation of learners-locals (who agreed on the necessity of this program and actively participated in it) in conducting the research did not diminish the significant role of the associates' previous knowledge and experience. Second, the experts' and associates' opinions on the classification of generative themes, based on the social sciences, outweighed those of the local population. Third, some experts were responsible for the breakdown of the content into units, while others made suggestions that were incorporated into the planning of the curriculum and/or were included in the short essays written on the subject (with bibliographical references suggested by experts). These short essays would constitute part of the material used to train the associates who participated in the "educational circles." In the curriculum planning procedure described in *Pedagogy of the Oppressed*, the role of the experts and associates was crucial, especially in the final phases.

The popular and democratic character of Freire's perspective for curriculum planning was based on the participants' direct involvement in the planning process and on the beliefs the lower classes held about social reality. These were the starting point for the selection of content, which was very similar to that of the pre-1964 literacy program.

At the end of the 1960s and for the duration of the 1970s, if we take into account the formations of various social and political forces, which on first sight indicated the strengthening of the lower social classes and strata in conjunction with the different versions of the political Left at an international level, the creation of the conditions for the development of curricula that would encompass similar goals and would adopt similar positions in order to define their content seemed possible. This could not be done within the context of the formal education system in countries where these social and political forces had not come to power; it could, however, be implemented within such a context in countries governed by these political forces. Freire's perspective on curriculum planning was formulated during his exiled years based on these two contexts, and its basic advantage was that it could be implemented in both.

This perspective is founded on the integral unity of its key elements, that is, the combination of a cultural-popular student-centered program, expressed through the curriculum content, and on a purely political conception-standpoint that supported the goals of the program that the experts and associates had to adopt during its planning process. Freire stresses the integral unity of these elements when he writes: "Because educator-educatee accept in communion with each other the role of subjects in the educational act, which is a permanent process, the educator no longer has the right to establish the curriculum-content of education, which does not belong to him exclusively. The organization of the curriculum, which must be regarded as a 'knowable object' by both educator-educatee and educatee-educator, requires the investigation of what we usually term the educatees' 'thematic universe'" (Freire 1972: 180–181). In defending the necessity of the teaching materials that were based on the generative themes in São Tomé at the end of his years in exile, Freire goes on to suggest that the opposite of manipulation was neither the illusion of neutrality nor of spontaneity but the critical and democratic participation of the learners in the process of acquiring knowledge. The subjects of this process should be the learners themselves.

The experience in Guinea-Bissau, where Freire supported the revolutionary government's political choice regarding the language of instruction, led to the failure of the implementation of his plans, which very clearly portrayed the relationship between the implementation of his perspective for curriculum planning and the formation of the correlation between social and political forces. As mentioned earlier, the strengthening of the lower social classes and the political forces of the Left was only temporary because their power was challenged and then gradually overturned in the 1980s. Thus, the popular-democratic perspective for curriculum planning formed by Freire within a specific framework of international power correlation will be called on to prove its value against a different and much more negative international background. The new period of Freire's work, marked by the return to his homeland in 1980 after sixteen years of exile, was affected by this change.

Freire returned to Brazil because democratization was beginning there, an outcome of mobilization mostly by the lower social classes that crystallized in the formation of new dynamic movements by workers and the landless, as well as other social movements, such as the feminist and black civil rights movements. In addition to this process of organization, the experience that both the intellectuals and the left-wing political groups had gained from their struggles against the imposed dictatorship, as well as the political marginalization of the orthodox Left in Brazil, constituted the basic driving forces for the creation of an original political subject-entity, the Workers Party (PT), with Freire one of its founding members.

In the 1980s, the PT grew quickly and had significant electoral success for several reasons: mainly its manifold relationships with the lower social classes, whose financial position, however, had deteriorated; an ethos of radicalism and denial of individualism; and the struggles for the essential democratization of the country. Of course, the coexistence of diverse political views and practices within the party's interior, which constituted the party's fundamental characteristic and enabled it to come into contact with a wide spectrum of social forces, could, at times, under certain circumstances, create problems of cohesion and effectiveness. Such problems were mainly expressed at a local level, where PT could not stabilize its electoral accomplishments. The municipality of São Paulo from 1989 until 1991, when Freire undertook the responsibility for educational reform, was one such case.

During the first years of the third period of his work, that is, from his return to Brazil until the initiation of educational reform in São Paulo (1980–1989), Freire readjusted his political views in relation to his previous periods, primarily based on the terms and conditions of the creation and development of PT. The Workers Party expressed a new political strategy with numerous similarities to his heterodox interpretation of Marxism. These similarities included a different approach to the issue of sociopolitical transformation when compared to that of the orthodox communist parties and disagreement with the regimes of so-called existing socialism in Eastern Europe. However, Freire did not identify fully with the PT interpretation, as the party did not have the characteristics of revolutionary liberation movements in countries already freed from the shackles of colonial rule, which theorists of the school of dependence considered to be vanguard.

Of PT's basic political priorities, which Freire adopted, he promoted mainly two political positions. The first was unity in diversity, a position that illustrated how PT had been formed by people from various social classes, strata, and political groups with very significant differences. This position had its roots in a new conceptualization of the oppressed, not as a social class but as a heterogeneous alliance of social groups with distinct characteristics that formed the cause of their oppression (race, gender, social class). This position reflected an acceptance that there was a wide range of forms of oppression and that these could not be reduced to class struggle. The second position consisted of enhancement and wide implementation of democracy, a political position that not only validated PT in the consciousness of many people, but also did not contradict what Freire had supported during his years in exile regarding the relationship between revolutionary leadership and the people because he did not approach it as a tactical position but as a fundamental ingredient of the socialist perspective.

According to Freire, these two positions should be viewed as the basic components of the rediscovery of power, which required an all-inclusive dialogue of all the issues relating to radical sociopolitical transformation, as well as the content of socialist transition. A meaningful popular democracy was the cornerstone of Freire's political thought. A meaningful popular democracy for those who fought for radical sociopolitical transformation would have to make clear, both in words and in action, that this position was not in opposition to the vision of socialism and that to identify it with forms of bourgeois democracy was a mistake.

These positions constituted a readjustment of Freire's political perspective during his exiled years in the context of Brazil's new conditions, but without changing the character of his political orientation. In other words, they constituted a nondecisive shift when compared to his positions in the previous period, a shift within continuity. This readjustment, apart from Freire's participation in PT, was also linked to the appearance and deepening of the crisis of the heterodox Marxist interpretation, reinforced by the challenge to the theoretical adequacy of the school of dependence and the political retreat of the radical liberation movements (after Mao's death and the final defeat of the Cultural Revolution in China). The crisis was part of a shift in the social, ideological, and political interrelationships of power in favor of the forces of capitalism and its political representatives at an international level, which arose in the 1980s.

A typical characteristic of the political readjustment Freire made during his years in exile in the context of Brazil's new conditions is illustrated by his abandonment of the viewpoint that the transition to socialism was extremely difficult in the rich countries of the West, a position supported by the school of dependence. Freire turned his attention to the developed world of the capitalist metropolis. He cooperated with U.S. educators with critical views as to the possibility of implementing a strategy of sociopolitical transformation in a large country (both financially and socially) such as Brazil. At the same time, he continued to zealously (but also critically) support the projects of socialist transformation in small nations, which, however, were becoming ever rarer.

Freire's return to Brazil intensified a need to define the type of intervention in the official school system championed by those who favored a socialist-oriented radical social and political transformation. The initiation of the democratization process in Brazil brought on a wave of optimism and support for intervention in the official school system that could, however, according to Freire, lead to illusions about the role of education. His collaboration with U.S. educators offered him the opportunity to utilize their analyses, which enabled him to conclude that the work within the schools and social movements had to be connected, so that the potential of education would not be naïvely overestimated. Its relationship to the social structure should not be misjudged, nor should its role be identified as simply reproducing the dominant ideology.

The intervention that Freire proposed was characterized by the promotion of popular education in the context of the official education system, which would include a struggle based on certain positions regarding the curriculum. Included in these positions were the following three: the starting point for the selection of the curriculum content would be based on participants' beliefs about social reality, the curriculum content would relate to the social context, and exclusionary viewpoints regarding curriculum content would be rejected. These positions could not make sense generally without acceptance that school is a site for social struggle, which is in contrast to Saviani's approach,[3] an approach that did not question the ways knowledge is produced nor its relationship to economic production and sociopolitical power relations.

Out of these three positions, the first two were included in the perspective Freire formed during his exiled years. In his 1980–1989 talking books, Freire's main attempt was to connect these two positions with the view that formal education was a site where the reproduction of the dominant ideology would be in direct struggle with its opposing view, namely, education for liberation. Furthermore, these two positions were viewed by Freire as the liberation project's basic elements for challenging the reproduction of the unimpeded dominant ideology. This, of course, did not mean that Freire envisioned the role of education as purely an ideological one.

In dealing with the issue of teaching the dominant linguistic norm, Freire shows that he was anything but indifferent to the needs of students' conditions of survival both at school and in society. He proposed fighting against school dropout and failure rates; this fight, coupled with the challenge to the dominant ideology, constituted the necessary ingredients for the struggle for popular education. Working-class students had to learn the elitist linguistic norm in order to survive and criticize it, despite the dangers of their being assimilated into the dominant logic that this instruction entailed. This could be achieved only through quality education, which the dominant class did not provide for the lower classes.

The third position, in which students had to study the fundamental theories of every discipline, did not contradict the two previous ones, because teachers were obliged to begin with the informal knowledge of the students and connect it to scientific knowledge, which would entail all the relevant classic theories of every discipline and allow students to understand them within the current social framework. In other words, the positions that the teachers had to adopt to promote popular education in the official school system were a readjustment to the perspective on curriculum planning Freire had developed during his exiled years.

The content of primary school curriculum planning during educational reform in São Paulo was also defined in terms of these three positions. The process of defining curriculum content on the basis of the students' beliefs about social reality was evident, because from these beliefs the important situations were derived, which in turn brought about generative themes. The teachers had to forge the connection of the curriculum to its social context. Connecting the generative themes to knowledge derived from various disciplines should not merely question the existence of strict boundaries between these disciplines, but should also adopt a critical approach to the way knowledge is socially produced and the way it contributes either to the reproduction of power relations or to the creation of new knowledge and a sociopolitical transformation. The rejection of exclusionary viewpoints from the curriculum content was evident in the definition of the generative theme as a way to knowledge, to the comprehension and intervention of a specific reality under study, which, among others, presupposed collective work, discussion, problematization, posing of questions, conflict, and participation—processes that do not comply with exclusionary viewpoints.

In the São Paulo program there was less emphasis on the relationship between knowledge and the subject's direct practical activity toward sociopolitical transformation than in the program presented in *Pedagogy of the Oppressed,* where generative themes were directly related to limiting situations. Apparently this was due to the different contexts in which the two programs were implemented. We should keep in mind that the earlier program was addressed to adults, whereas the São Paulo program in-volved children, and that the dropout and school failure rates were huge at the primary school level in the municipality of São Paulo. As a result, we can assume that the pressure to meet basic schoolwork demands meant that there were limited possibilities for immediate, practical sociopolitical activity outside the school environment.

As far as the goals of the program were concerned, the radical sociopolitical transformation with a socialist orientation constituted the central political goal; the central educational goal was the promotion of popular education in Brazil. For Freire, popular education included the creation of critical consciousness (i.e., the educational goal of the earlier program) by means of opposition to the dominant ideology; such education also spoke to an increase in the number of lower-social-class children attending school and to the fight against school failure through the provision of quality education. We can therefore conclude that curriculum planning in São Paulo was derived from a readjustment of Freire's positions during his years of exile on curriculum goals and definition of content.

Let me note here that in both the earlier and the São Paulo programs, Freire did not adopt the idea of specialists with unlimited power. He was in favor of a process that was collectively developed by teachers, students, parents, school committees, education specialists from the municipality, schools, and universities, and that included contributions from the social movements. Even though students participated in program planning along with other agents, this did not mean that their role was equal to that of the experts and associates of the program (who in this case did not involve researchers but only teachers, who undertook the bulk of the research as well as the teaching).

The fact that the entire school staff participated in the initial research into the important situations of the school community did not mean that the teachers, in cooperation with the municipality staff, did not play an important role, given their expertise and experience. Moreover, it was teachers who, after investigating the key issues of the school community, worked collectively to produce one generative theme for each school semester. These generative themes constituted the basis for the curriculum.

Moreover, the knowledge and experience of educators played a decisive role in the process of connecting the generative themes to the disciplines, as well as in the process of formulating the generative questions. Educators were further assisted in their responsibilities by the work of municipality experts, who provided them with supporting materials such as brief histories of certain disciplines. The role of the subjects in the planning process of the São Paulo curriculum was similar to that of the subjects involved in Freire's program while in exile, because the role of the program experts and associates there was also crucial.

The same applies to the planning process; it was contingent on the investigation phases of the generative themes, the choice of topic, and its connection to the knowledge related to the disciplines. Although the process presented in *Pedagogy of the Oppressed* included essentially the same phases, the main difference was the additional phase of experimental implementation, which contributed to the selection of themes. The combination of the cultural-popular student-centeredness, which put the students at the center of curriculum planning without ignoring their wider community, and the political and educational goals of the program that had to be adopted by the experts and associates during program planning constituted key characteristics of this perspective and were founded on the integral unity of these two elements. At this juncture, it is safe to conclude that because the goals, the positions on the definition of content, the process, and the role of the subjects were similar, the popular-democratic perspective on curriculum planning that Freire had developed during his exiled years is the perspective on which the reform in São Paulo primary schools was based.

Freire's perspective on curriculum planning achieved positive results in a different framework from that envisioned during his exile. That is, of course, if we assume that the implementation of the Interdisciplinary Project contributed positively to the São Paulo reform in the increase of student participation in schools as well as in the reduction in the school failure rates. This assumption is well founded because the democratization of the administration, teacher-training courses, changes in assessment procedures, improvements to the infrastructure, and the introduction of computers in education would have been highly unlikely to achieve these results if there had been no curriculum reform.

In the six years between the São Paulo education reform and Freire's death in 1997, there was no radical change in his political positions. His more open criticism of orthodox Marxism, as interpreted by the so-called existing socialist regimes, and his assertion that he did not consider class struggle to be the sole driving force of history, cannot be considered a radical change. Freire continued to support the strategic value of democracy as a founding element of a radical sociopolitical transformation with a socialist orientation that was related to the rediscovery of power, unity within the context of diversity, the necessity of a new relationship between the people and the party; the latter should not be centrally organized as a vanguard party but as a party of the masses. Moreover, the starting point for the definition of curriculum content based on people's beliefs about social reality, his position about connecting the curriculum content with the social framework, and his position on rejecting exclusionary viewpoints from curriculum content are reiterated in his texts written after the São Paulo reform.

THE DIFFERENTIATION AND CONTEMPORARY VALUE OF FREIRE'S PERSPECTIVE

By the end of the nineteenth century, the traditional perspective dominated the curriculum in the United States. It aimed at maintaining the existing organization of a society that was founded on an established economic and political liberalism. Along these lines, curriculum content was to center on the classical Western tradition, that is, subjects such as Greek, Latin, and Geometry, which were considered appropriate for the development of rational thought. Faculty psychology, according to which the brain resembled a muscle that developed with exercise, contributed to the definition of curriculum content. As a consequence, the planning process was primarily the task of experts in the aforementioned disciplines.[4]

At the dawn of the twentieth century, however, economic and social changes were enormous. The Unites States had already transformed from a rural into an industrial society, internal and external migration resulted in the creation of big cities, and there was an enormous concentration of production and wealth as expressed by growing corporate mergers that signaled a key process, that is, the transition to monopolistic capitalism.

These changes, of course, cannot be disarticulated from the class struggles that constituted a visible danger to the ruling class. The configuration of power correlations between capital and labor forces resulted in the division of the first three decades of the century in two periods: a period of reforms, the so-called Progressive era (1900–1918), and a period of increasing capital profitability, intensity of social and political oppression, and empowerment of conservative ideas, the so-called golden age (1918–1929), which was interrupted by the Great Depression.

Progressive education was a movement for educational reform whose beginning and development were associated with the changes and conflicts just mentioned. It was expressed in many different domains of the educational process, and its basic political orientation was the creation of a society characterized by harmony, economic stability, and growth, an "organic" society where the interests of both capital and labor would coincide.[5] Until the 1930s, four perspectives on curriculum planning were put forward, revised versions of which are still formulated: a social efficiency perspective, a child-centered perspective, Dewey's perspective, and a social reconstruction perspective.

The perspective of social efficiency was first formulated by Bobbit at the beginning of the golden age in 1918, and it marked the creation of the field of curriculum studies in the United States. Drawing from Thorndike's behaviorism, Ross's approach of social control, and Taylor's scientific management, Bobbit formed a perspective, which became the basis for Tyler's rationale as well as B. Bloom and Mager's propositions, that largely influenced postwar views and practices on curriculum planning. This perspective was founded on the political goal of increasing the efficiency of the existing capitalist socioeconomic organization by means of reducing waste, and on the educational goal of enabling peoples' adjustment to this organization. As its departure point for the definition of the curriculum content, this perspective included the formulation of concise, clear, and detailed educational objectives that had to correspond to adult activities whose achievement could be measured. Curriculum planning was an issue to be dealt with by the experts, who, starting from the definition of objectives, had to design relevant series of experiences for the learners by using scientific/objective processes.[6]

The social efficiency perspective differs from Freire's in that its political goal is contrary to sociopolitical transformation with a socialist direction, and its educational goal is opposed to the formation of a critical consciousness. Social efficiency employs a starting point for the definition of curriculum content that does not take into consideration the ways learners perceive social reality, and ultimately this view espouses the absolute domination of the experts in the planning process, whose decisions are thought to be sociopolitically neutral.

Considerable differences exist between Freire's perspective and the child-centered perspective on curriculum planning formulated, mainly, by Hall at the end of the nineteenth century. This perspective was founded on the individualism of the liberal upper middle class, whose members were indifferent to social problems and social injustices. They were instead interested in everyday material comforts and their own children's success, as Counts wrote at the end of the 1920s during which child-centered practices had been reinforced in the field of curriculum.[7] The political goal of this perspective, clearly antithetical to the radical sociopolitical transformation with a socialist direction, has a romantic character. The two perspectives also differ in their educational goals: natural development of the child versus critical consciousness. Moreover, the starting point for the definition of the curriculum content on the basis of the child's natural impulses is different from dependence on the learners' beliefs about social reality. In other words, in the framework of the child-centered perspective, the child is perceived as a totality of natural inclinations, which is radically different from the cultural-popular student-centeredness found in Freire's perspective. Freire's political goals and positions have nothing in common with those of the child-centered perspective.

I have already referred in Chapter 1 and earlier in this chapter to the relationship between Freire's and Dewey's positions about the political goals of the curriculum. Comparing the two educators' perspectives, we can draw several conclusions. First, the political goals of the two perspectives are oppositional because Freire supports radical sociopolitical transformation with a socialist direction, whereas Dewey supports the expansion of democracy to every sector of culture combined with the development and diffusion of scientific thought and the planned coordination of industrial growth. Whereas for the Brazilian educator radical sociopolitical transformation is directly related to changes in social structures and relationships, the American liberal educator and pragmatist philosopher does not transcend the boundaries of reforms that converge in building a harmonious society of economic stability and growth, that is, a society where there would be no sociopolitical conflicts, an "organic" society. Based on the foregoing political goals, Freire sets the formation of a critical consciousness as the educational goal of his curriculum; for Dewey it is adjustment to existing social functions and peoples' contribution to reform of the socioeconomic and political regime.

Second, Freire's perspective involves the unity of the cultural-popular student-centeredness and the clearly political character of programs goals. The experts and associates undertake the task of relating the ways people understand social reality and, more specifically, their less controlled empirical knowledge to more rigorous scientific knowledge. Dewey's perspective entails another kind of unity, one between what is considered to be a child's natural inclinations (social predisposition, inclination to constructions, discovery and experimentation, expression) and expert knowledge on disciplines and social occupations that serve basic human needs. Both perspectives approach the problem of the definition of the curriculum content and its organization on the basis of the unity of two elements, that is, on the basis of a relationship; however, the poles of the relationship are different.

In addition, even though the role of experts and associates is important in both perspectives, they nevertheless differ greatly. In Freire, the choice and reorganization of themes by the experts and associates are influenced by the ways students perceive social reality and their participation in the thematic investigation. In Dewey, in contrast, the experts are influenced only by their own perception of the children's natural inclinations.[8] Therefore, it is obvious that the two approaches are disparate, despite Dewey's initial influences on Freire and even though specific pedagogic views were shaped from elements from both frameworks.[9]

I will conclude this comparison with a reference to the social reconstructive perspective. The exclusive dependence on teachers and experts, who would play a decisive role in the creation of an education that would be a key to social change, characterized the perspective of social reconstruction. This perspective had been initially expressed by Ward's adherence to the importance of cultural capital distribution through education in order to achieve social progress. Counts, the most important representative of this perspective, also espoused this position when he stated his belief that teachers could lead social reform by representing not the interests of the moment or of a social class, but rather of the people, thus converting education into a force of social rebirth and schools into centers for study and for the creation of a new culture. Brameld, a postwar representative of social reconstructionism, also supported these ideas and claimed that the common goal of all proposals for social reform was the establishment of state planning that had to work if people desired cultural rebirth. Basically, Brameld assigned the work of implementing this planning and guidance of modern citizens to experts, in the direction of social self-realization.

The social reconstruction perspective on curriculum planning challenged the conservative political goals of the child-centered and the social efficiency perspectives as well as the inefficacy and the inhumane nature of capitalism after the Great Depression. It stressed the dangers of the complete destruction of culture in the postwar era and suggested that technology should be free of restrictions or claims to any kind of privilege, as well as serving the popular masses by means of a production and distribution system. However, as far as its political and educational goals were concerned, social reconstruction did not transcend the boundaries of the progressive education movement that had generated it. It did, of course, extend the boundaries of social reform that progressive education required in a period of socioeconomic crisis, during which Dewey favored a radical reform of economic structures in the United States. Broadening the curriculum content to refer not only to all aspects of modern society but also to the solution of social problems in the direction of creating a new culture constituted the starting point for the definition of curriculum content in the context of the social reconstruction perspective.[10] The organization of curriculum content on the basis of themes often creates confusion between progressive ideas and Freire's perspective, in which the curriculum is constructed on the basis of generative themes.[11]

However, extending the boundaries of social reform and the corresponding position of broadening the curriculum content does not imply that the difference between Freire's perspective and social reconstruction, evident mainly in the latter's dependence on teachers and experts, is refuted. Politically, of course, social reconstruction is closer to Freire's than Dewey's ideas or those of social efficiency and child-centeredness. Nevertheless, Freire's perspective on curriculum planning differs significantly from the ones developed by the progressive education movement.

Comparing perspectives on curriculum planning formulated in the United States during the postwar era is easier than comparing those developed in the first forty years of the twentieth century, the reason being that the latter were expressed in revised versions after the war as well, thus occupying an important place in modern theory and practice in this field. For instance, the traditional perspective will find its successors in the work of Adler, A. Bloom, and Hirsch. Tyler, B. Bloom and Mager, and the representatives of "life adjustment education" will follow the theoretical starting points of Bobbit's social efficiency perspective. The followers of the child-centered perspective will use similar positions to the ones used at the beginning of the century in ventures of alternative schools. Brameld will revise the social reconstruction perspective, and Dewey's ideas will be utilized in the planning of curricula based on action research and school experimentations such as the Coalition of Essential Schools.[12]

The new phase of postwar capitalist development in the United States resulted in the differentiation of the labor force and the transition of part of it to skilled service work. The main characteristics of this development were capital accumulation, decline of traditional industry, rapid technological growth, and its use in capitalist production. This development, alongside the expansion of the international economic, political, ideological, and military influence of the United States, did not occur without conflicts. New versions of the social efficiency perspective for curriculum planning facilitated the basic objective of the dominant social forces, which was to form a social and educational consensus aimed at a closer connection between education and capitalist development, as well as a more effective control of education based on a common framework and evaluation standards that demanded a curriculum with a wide scope but little depth.[13]

With the launching of *Sputnik* at the end of the 1950s, the dominant sociopolitical forces experienced a shock that initiated the appearance of another perspective. This one attempted to satisfy the criticism of American academics about the devaluing of certain disciplines; basically, this perspective attempted to comply with the government's redefinition of education as a national defense issue, as well as establish a national curriculum framework that would emphasize technology, mathematics, and the sciences.[14] Based on the findings of the 1959 Woods Hall conference, Bruner founded this perspective of curriculum planning.

Bruner's perspective was based on the political goal of adapting education to the new needs of capitalist development and empowering the United States in the cold war competition. The whole student population was seen as a reservoir from which some could work their way up to the top of the scientific and technological communities. Bruner's view resonated with the goal of improving teaching effectiveness by approaching the student as a scientist who had to actively participate in understanding the basic structures of each discipline. In this way, students could become useful to the United States in assuming the leading international roles at economic, military, political, and cultural levels.

The emphasis on learning the structure of disciplines was a necessary precondition for success, and it constituted the starting point for the definition of curriculum content. The position according to which it is possible to teach the basic principles of all subjects to all students of all ages in an appropriate form was at the core of content organization and led to the design of a spiral curriculum that examined in depth the structures of disciplines. Research could trigger the interest of "gifted" students without discouraging those "less favored by nature." The role of the academics who had expertise in the disciplines became dominant in curriculum planning.[15]

Even though programs based on student learning of the structure of disciplines included humanistic elements as well as development of a research spirit and active learning, it is obvious that this perspective differs from that of Freire.[16] Once more, the political goal of radical sociopolitical transformation with a socialist orientation is opposed to the adaptation of education to meet the needs of capitalist development. Along the same lines, defining the curriculum content by relying on the structure of the disciplines is radically different from departing from the students' beliefs about social reality as expressed by Freire. Finally, the significant role of the experts and associates in Freire's planning process cannot be compared to the authority of the expert scientists, who are almost exclusively responsible for curriculum planning in Bruner's perspective.

The development of the research spirit and active learning that characterized Bruner's perspective resembled Dewey's ideas, which resulted in expanding its influence. Moreover, the emphasis on the structures of disciplines did not contradict the postwar versions of social efficiency. Similarly, because of common political goals, the criticism of Bruner's perspective on curriculum planning by followers of Piaget's psychology did not mean that these two perspectives were oppositional.[17] Again, Freire's perspective is different from the one adopted by the Swiss psychologist and epistemologist, because the educational goal of his perspective is the achievement of a more effective learning without challenging the dominant sociopolitical and educational priorities, and the definition of the curriculum content in terms of the students' knowledge is concerned with the knowledge of the subject to be taught. In Freire's perspective, in contrast, the generative themes, which constitute the basic components of the curriculum content, are defined according to the outcomes of the research on the students' beliefs about social reality, a process in which the students themselves participate.

After the 1960s, no other radically different perspective on curriculum planning developed in the United States beyond those presented earlier. In the 1960s, learning the structure of disciplines was significantly enforced, because it had full support and federal government funding. The federal government mainly turned to university projects for the instruction of subjects such as physics, mathematics, chemistry, and biology. The movement for the reform of the national curriculum focused on the alignment of secondary education subjects to the academic fields of the university and the establishment of academic rigor in schools. In order to achieve this, the control of the curriculum had to be removed from educators. It was the beginning of a process that was to continue in the next decades, and at its core was a shift in emphasis from local attempts to change the curriculum to a centrally controlled reform. In other words, this process enforced the role of the central political authority in controlling school curricula throughout the country; one result was the appearance and expansion of the use of so-called teacher-proof curricula.

However, the 1960s were a decade of controversy and social struggles in the United States. The movements for the social and political rights of black people and women and the movement of youth contestation and opposition to the Vietnam War had shaken the nation. During the same decade and in line with wider social, political, and ideological disputes and searches for alternative solutions, curriculum formation was called into question.

The dominant behaviorism and scientism received the first heterogeneous attacks, which culminated in criticism over the static and limited character of the field. Criticism on educational operations first came to light alongside a radical increase of interest in versions of progressive education and research, and in pedagogic practices that were connected to it, such as action research, in Marxism, in humanistic psychology, in reform of the legacy in the history of education, and in the relations of all these to the theory and practice of curriculum studies. At the beginning of the 1970s, it was widely accepted that the field was undergoing a crisis. The so-called reconceptualization of the field came as a result of the culture of critique that had been developing. It came at a time when the importance of the work on planning, implementing, and evaluating the curriculum as a guide for those working in schools was seriously downplayed, and there was an attempt to use the work done in the humanities (history, philosophy, and literary criticism). I deem the term *reconceptualization of the field* somewhat exaggerated because the core issues that established the field did not change. Therefore, I use the term *movement for the reconceptualization* of the curriculum field, which does not underestimate the relevant confrontations briefly mentioned here and does not imply that the curriculum field underwent radical transformation after 1970.

The movement for the reconceptualization came under severe criticism for its relation to the radical anticulture of the 1960s and for its lack of interest in the curriculum. Nonetheless, reconceptualization did not mark the disappearance of traditional work. Schools were increasingly controlled by businessmen, politicians, bureaucrats, and "social engineers," who mostly attempted to adjust them to the neoliberal and neoconservative doctrines that dominated during and following the 1980s by taking advantage of the consequences of the economic crisis and the political weakness of the social movements. In the absence of any political will to deal with the issue, experts in the curriculum field tried to remove it from schools and focused on comprehending its complexity. Even though the already loosely connecting bonds of the reconceptualization movement were declining, its influence on the formation of the field was considerable, and it could be traced in new ways of comprehending the curriculum: as a political, racial, phenomenological, poststructuralist, deconstructed, postmodern, autobiographical-biographical, aesthetic, theological, and international text, as well as a text of social gender.[18] At this point, we can note the following concerning Freire's influence on U.S. educators who played a significant role in the curriculum field: as I have shown, the Brazilian educator's perspective on curriculum planning, first expressed in *Pedagogy of the Oppressed* (which was published in English at the beginning of the 1970s), was explicitly different from the other already expressed perspectives in the United States.

Given the social, political, and ideological contestation at the end of the 1960s and the beginning of the 1970s and the quest for potential alternative solutions, as well as the crisis in defining curriculum content and the emergence of the movement for the reconceptualization of the curriculum field, the conditions were ripe for the emergence of a different perspective. Besides, even if we assume that any reverberation of the projects of the Sunday Socialist Schools at the beginning of the century had been lost,[19] the ground had been prepared by other projects related to the social movements of the 1960s.

Elias mentions that the pedagogy of the Mississippi Freedom Schools in the 1960s bears many similarities to Freire's pedagogy (Elias 1973: 81). The purpose of these schools was to provide educational experiences to students so that they could question the myths of society, understand its realities more clearly, and find alternatives as well as new directions for action. These schools emphasized the use of questions and discussion circles where students would discuss their everyday lives and the conditions of their oppression. The Freedom School curriculum content consisted in comparing the students' reality with that of others, examining reality and the power structure, and investigating the lives of poor black and poor white people.

Therefore, Freire's perspective was relevant to the formation of an ongoing political and educational dialogue in the United States in the early 1970s; its popular-democratic character influenced educators such as Huebner, Greene, Macdonald, Pinar, Apple, Penna, Anyon, Popkewitz, Lundgren and Aronowitz,[20] who contributed to the formation of the curriculum field in this developed capitalist country. Giroux has acknowledged Freire's significant influence in his contribution to the movement for the reconceptualization of the field. According to McLaren's review of Giroux's work, this influence can be traced in his work during the late 1970s and early 1980s (McLaren 1988, xiii–xv). Giroux combined Freire's influence with other perspectives and formulated a theoretical approach that, as we have already seen, also influenced Freire. However, an examination of specific types of Freire's influence on U.S. educators who contributed to the formation of the curriculum field extends beyond the scope of this study.

In conclusion, we can say that Freire's perspective comprises the following: (a) a central political goal that is radical sociopolitical transformation with a socialist orientation and a corresponding educational goal that is the formation of critical consciousness, perceived as a liberation act (critique of the lived experiences and collective effort to transcend them); (b) a definition of curriculum content based on the students' beliefs about social reality, on a linking of knowledge to the wider social context, on the unity between theory and practice, on a rejection of any possible exclusion of viewpoints, and on generative themes as the basis for the organization of the curriculum content; (c) a collective participation of all subjects directly or indirectly involved in the process of curriculum planning, with an emphasis on the role of teachers, researchers, and experts in the program; and (d) a structuring of the planning process in three phases: investigation of the thematic universe of the students and their community, selection and codification of generative themes, and a relating of generative themes to knowledge from relevant disciplines.

The elements in Freire's perspective that offer the theoretical and practical adequacy of an important perspective in the curriculum studies field and that provide a fertile ground for those teachers and others involved in the struggle for the formation of a new sociopolitical majority, which can open the way for a radical transformation of contemporary societies with a democratic socialist orientation, are as follows:

1. Freire's perspective is founded on the close relationship between cultural and popular student-centeredness (illustrated in the fact that curriculum content is based and depends on the students' beliefs about and perceptions of social reality) and central political and educational goals that provide an answer to the mechanistic transmission of predetermined knowledge.

2. Freire's perspective approaches the relation between sociopolitical transformation and education without fetishizing the importance of one or the other pole of this equation. Freire sees education itself as a site of conflict and struggle between two kinds of labor: one that consciously or unconsciously, in one way or another, aims at reproducing the dominant ideology; another that promotes a questioning of the dominant ideology. This perception of education serves as an answer to both determinism and voluntarism.

3. The curriculum in Freire's perspective is not something disengaged from the social and political struggles inside and outside education. The definition of the character of each curricular component and, of course, of the curriculum as a totality has an influence on power correlations, which determine educational functions and outcomes. Curriculum planning is an explicitly political process.

4. Freire's perspective differs considerably from those born in the context of the progressive education movement, a movement that marked the history of pedagogic ideas and the initial formation of the curriculum field. It rejects the futile spontaneity of child-centered approaches, the

apparent conservatism of social efficiency, Dewey's commitment to the liberal ideals of social harmony, and the naïve faith of the followers of social reconstructionism in the absolute power of education. In other words, although Freire's perspective distances itself from those components of progressive education that opposed traditional education, it does employ some of this movement's ideas (such as the promotion of the rights of the learners for active participation in every part of the educational process) by placing them in a different context of curriculum planning, thus giving them a different content.

5. Freire's perspective on curriculum planning develops the Marxist ideas on polytechnic education, the connection between scientific/technical education and an understanding of production processes, the designation of labor as one of the main sources of knowledge, and the promotion of the values of solidarity and social responsibility in order to give meaning to the notion of radical sociopolitical transformation with a democratic socialist orientation as well as to the relation of education to this transformation. Freire's view also uses critical evaluations of the causes that led socialist projects to collapse, proposing a form of socialist transition where substantial democracy, unity in diversity, and radical transformations in the superstructure will be interlinked to changes in the relations of production. This socialist transition would include active social and political subjects and would be expressed in the form not only of a purely social and political revolution, but also of a cultural one.

Freire's perspective is popular, radical, and democratic. It remains timely, oppositional to the dominant perspective used in the context of neoliberal and neoconservative educational reform, because no one has yet convincingly proved that the character of modern societies has changed radically, despite proclamations by the preachers of fabricated arguments for the arrival of the end of history. The dominant mode of production continues to be capitalist and to characterize modern societies, despite the important economic, technological, social, political, and cultural changes in the last decades. Freire's perspective, born in the second half of a century that was marked by competition between capitalist and socialist orientations (in all the forms that this competition took), does not belong to the past, because there is no evidence that this competition has ended. On the contrary, its manifold reproductions appear in current sociopolitical contrasts and conflicts. In this sense, Freire's perspective is important nowadays for those teachers and curriculum specialists who both theoretically and practically challenge the dominant assumptions of curriculum planning with one precondition: that its critical theoretical reexamination and its creative practical development will not constitute mere rhetorical commitments.

ENDNOTES

⟜

NOTES TO FOREWORD

1. Paulo Freire, *A sombra desta mangueira* [*Pedagogy of the Heart*] (São Paulo: Editora Olho d'Água, 2000), 25.

2. Nita Freire, "Emancipatory Education: Paulo Freire's Influence on Global Citizenship" (lecture given at the University of Alberta, Edmonton, Canada, October 2008).

3. Ibid.

4. *Time Magazine*, March 9, 2009, 11.

5. Paulo Freire, *Pedagogy of Freedom: Ethics, Democracy, and Civic Courage* (Boulder, CO: Rowman and Littlefield, 1998), 116–117.

6. Ibid.

7. Henry A. Giroux, "Memory's Hope: In the Shadow of Paulo Presence" (unpublished manuscript, February 7, 2007).

8. Paulo Freire, *A educação na cidade* [*Pedagogy of the City*] (São Paulo: Cortez Editora, 1991), 14–15.

9. Ana Maria Saul in Paulo Freire, *Pedagogy of the City* (New York: Continuum, 1993), 150.

10. Freire, *Pedagogy of the City*, 19.

11. This issue is taken up in greater detail in Henry A. Giroux and Susan Searls Giroux, "Beyond Bailouts: On the Politics of Education After Neoliberalism," *Truthout*, December 31, 2008, www.truthout.org/123108; and in Henry A. Giroux and Ken Saltman, "Obama's Betrayal of Education," *Truthout*, December 17, 2008, http://www.truthout.org/121708R.

12. See Henry A. Giroux, *Against the Terror of Neoliberalism* (Boulder, CO: Paradigm Publishers, 2008).

13. Fulvia Carnevale and John Kelsey, "Art of the Possible: An Interview with Jacques Rancière," *Artforum* (March 2007): 264.

14. Frank Rich, "No Time for Poetry," *New York Times,* January 25, 2009.

15. Sheldon Wolin, *Democracy, Inc.: Managed Democracy and the Specter of Inverted Totalitarianism* (Princeton, NJ: Princeton University Press, 2008), 260–261.

16. Ibid., 261.

17. Zygmunt Bauman, *Liquid Life* (London: Polity Press, 2005), 14.

18. Sally Kohn, "Real Change Happens Off-Line," *Christian Science Monitor,* June 30, 2008, www.csmonitor.com/2008/0630/p09s01-coop.html.

19. Jacques Derrida, "Intellectual Courage: An Interview," trans. Peter K.

20. Freire, *Pedagogy of Freedom,* 116.

NOTES TO INTRODUCTION

1. I am comparing Freire's perspective with those formed and developed in the United States during the twentieth century so that I can reach solid conclusions. I do not underestimate the development of the curriculum field in other countries. However, there is one main reason that justifies this choice: curriculum theory and practice are widely debated in the United States, because of the historical formation of its political and educational systems. The two did not, as a rule, hinder educational innovations in a direct way, nor did they restrict curriculum decisionmaking to the central political power, at least until the end of the 1950s. For more details on the diversity of experimentation in U.S. public schools at the beginning of the twentieth century, see Reese 2000: 276–281.

2. The most significant and representative part of Freire's texts has been translated into English (Mayo 2004: 9–10). As for the quality of the translation from Portuguese into English, Freire himself never accepted the criticism of the English translation of his most popular book, *Pedagogy of the Oppressed,* even twenty years after its publication (Borg and Mayo 2000). This does not mean that the obstacle of the Portuguese language does not restrict my study. The use of translated texts that cover the entire chronological extent of Freire's work is essential. As Roberts (2000: 30–33) stresses, the biggest "mistake" in the study of Freire is that researchers focus their interest on his first essays without paying relevant attention to the many texts he wrote in the last phase of his work.

My criteria for defining the stages of Freire's work are based on the changes in his political positions, which include a decisive shift in his political orientation and then a readjustment of his subsequent political positions without further change in his political orientation. In each period, his positions on curriculum planning are related mainly to his political positions. These positions are directly associated with changes in economic, social, ideological, and political power dynamics and the resulting conflicts, primarily in the countries where his action and thought developed. Of course, I give emphasis to the Brazilian social context since Brazil was Freire's homeland and the place where his thoughts and actions were initially formed and in time finalized.

I examine Freire's political positions in order to extract the central political goal of his perspective on curriculum planning and relate that to his perspective's central educational goal. Distinguishing the two does not imply that the latter lacks political character. The central political goal of his perspective is the intended (via the curriculum) sociopolitical organization; the central educational goal is the intended impact of the curriculum on the subjects (mainly the students) as a means to achieve the central political goal.

NOTES TO CHAPTER 1

1. According to Jerez and Hernandez-Pico, Julião's and Freire's ideological formation were alike (Jerez and Hernandez-Pico 1973: 45–47).
2. See Coben 1998: 59.
3. In 1961, the Communist Party of Brazil changed its name to the Brazilian Communist Party with a view to supporting its legalization and promoting more efficiently the peaceful transition to socialism. The old name would be used in the future by a group of Maoists after they broke away from the party (Alexander 1999: 69–70).
4. "Militant democracy" is Mannheim's term.
5. The discovery card comprised diagrams with combinations of consonants and vowels resulting from an analysis of three-syllable generative words in Portuguese.

NOTES TO CHAPTER 2

1. She published many of Freire's works in Chile. Also, as Mayo mentions, she was a close collaborator of his who introduced him to the writings of Antonio Gramsci (Mayo 1997: 366). As for Gramsci's influence on Freire's work, see Mayo 1999: 7–8.
2. This conference is considered the culmination of the movement of liberation theology, which developed with the consent of Pope John XXIII (1958–1963) and the Second Vatican Council (1961–1965). Freire's ideas influenced the decisions of the bishops in Medellín, Colombia, who supported the pursuit of a new type of society and a new educational process. Their aim was to create individuals who would become the subjects of their own development, would be aware of their own

dignity, would self-define, and would develop a sense of communion. These decisions were considered by many to be the first step by conservative Catholic leaders to keep a distance from considering education to be a means of protecting the church and facilitating many Catholic educators' move toward liberation education (Coben 1998: 60; La Belle 1976: 341–342).

3. Whenever Freire referred to the concept of love, he would cite a quotation from the letter Che Guevara wrote to Carlos Guijano: "Let me tell you, at the risk of appearing ridiculous, that the genuine revolutionary is animated by feelings of love. It is impossible to imagine an authentic revolutionary without this quality" (cited in Freire 1999b: 43).

4. Many views have been expressed about how *Pedagogy of the Oppressed* and Freire's work in general have been influenced by certain philosophical theories. For one of many, see Aronowitz 1993: 12–18.

5. Freire acknowledged Hegel's influence on his definition of the concept of oppression and also underlined the importance of Hegel's influence on Marx by repeating Lenin's view that it is impossible to understand Marx without understanding Hegel (Torres 1998: 92).

6. According to Allman, Freire contributed quite significantly to Marxist thought. In *Pedagogy of the Oppressed* Freire explains how socialist educators and political activists can work with the people so that the latter can think critically or dialogically about their reality. In Allman's view, readings of *Pedagogy of the Oppressed* usually ignore that it refers to revolutionary strategy (Allman 1994: 144–161).

7. According to Torres, Freire's ideas were already implemented well before 1970 in many countries in Latin America (Uruguay, Argentina, Mexico, Chile, Peru, and Ecuador) on either a small or a large scale (Torres 1993: 123). English-speaking educators in the United States, according to Collins, started becoming acquainted with Freire's ideas in 1968 after an introductory paper written by Sanders (Collins 1973: 17).

8. These essays are "Cultural Action and Conscientization" and "The Adult Literacy Process as Cultural Action for Freedom."

9. In Guinea-Bissau thirty different languages and dialects were used. Creole had been developed gradually as a lingua franca combining African languages and Portuguese. According to Freire, it was a beautiful language as rich as the Portuguese language.

10. As Macedo mentions, the mistake of choosing Portuguese, the language of the colonizers, as the language of instruction was also repeated in the case of Cape Verde (Macedo 1991: 147–159). Furthermore, Galli and Jones argue that the use of Portuguese was one of the reasons that elitism was promoted in Guinea-Bissau education during the five-year period 1978–1983 (Galli and Jones 1987: 164–169). As a result, there was a reduction in student enrolment in the elementary four-year education at the same time that there was a dramatic increase in the number of

secondary education students. Also, the aggregate number of children of school age attending any form of education declined.

11. Freire had this dialogue with Antonio Faundez in August 1984 in Geneva (Freire and Faundez 1992: 141).

12. When Gleeson criticizes Freire's overemphasis on the power of education, he does not take into consideration all the texts Freire produced during this period (Gleeson 1974: 35).

13. Crawford argues that in *Pedagogy in Process*, Freire proposes a totally Marxist approach to the organization of society: workers united in common productive work aimed at abolishing the dichotomy between intellectual and manual work, farmers' cooperatives functioning on the basis of decisions made by the people, a government devoted to the people, and an economic system led by the values of usefulness rather than those of exchange (Crawford 1980: 67).

14. According to Allman, Freire's dialectic theory of consciousness was less explicit than his ontological position. His theory of consciousness and his dialectic understanding of reality were influenced by Marx's theoretical work (Allman 1997: 113–114).

15. When negotiating the concepts of "real" and "potential" consciousness, Freire refers to Lucien Goldman. According to Malcolm, Freire draws on Karl Jasper's ideas to define the concept of limit-situations. Freire approaches limit-situations not as the borderline between existence and nonexistence but as the borderline between to exist and to "exist more" (Malcolm 1999: 87)

16. Frankenstein and Powell emphasize the difference between Freire's theory of knowledge and positivism and his positions that knowledge is not static and never complete (Frankenstein and Powell 1994: 75–76). Knowledge is a product emerging from the interaction between human consciousness and reality and is related to the unity of subjectivity and objectivity and to the unity of practice and reflection, that is, praxis, which is not neutral.

NOTES TO CHAPTER 3

1. The armed struggle against the military coup was conducted both in the cities and the countryside. However, it was not massive, even though it succeeded in releasing political prisoners. For more details, see Wright and Wolford 2003: 5–6.

2. According to reports published in 1998, MST managed to organize nine hundred primary schools with eighty-five thousand students and twenty-five hundred teachers. Even though a big part of the content of the curriculum was similar to that of traditional public schools, the experience of the struggles brought about the need for a new school that would use a new pedagogy based on the work of Freire, Gramsci, Marx, and José Martí, the

Cuban revolutionary leader. For example, some of the pedagogical principles recorded in documents of the movement are as follows: the curriculum is founded on the problems that the school community faces, the political and educational procedures should be organically related to each other, education should be related to production, there has to be a democratic management of schools, and students should be self-organized (Kane 2000: 41–47).

3. Freire's political ideas were considered to be catalytic for the formation of PT (Gibson 1994: 39).

4. For example, his ideas were put into practice in Scotland at the end of the 1970s. For more details, see Kirkwood and Kirkwood 1989.

5. Freire had visited Chile several times during Salvador Allende's presidency (1970–1973). His last visit, a few months before the military coup, would be unforgettable because it taught him many things about the class struggle (Freire 1999b: 186–187).

6. For an analysis of dependence theory, compared and contrasted with the approach of modernization in Latin America during the first postwar decades and the 1980s, see Leonard 1990: 98–115.

7. Mayo notes that during a conference session in Chicago in 1991, Freire argued that one cannot reduce all forms of oppression to the class struggle (Mayo 1994: 138–139).

8. Freire's pedagogy was criticized for lacking a certain feminist examination of disputes between oppressed groups (Weiler 1991: 449–474). Findlay, however, while arguing for the versatility of Freire's work on social movements, stressed that his pedagogic precepts aimed at revealing the sources of oppression and social rivalries (Findlay 1994: 118). Findlay also argued that this kind of work was to be done within social movements, which unavoidably constituted unstable amalgams of differentiated groups.

9. According to Freire, his acquaintance with Giroux's texts started two or three years before his return to Brazil, that is at the end of the 1970s, and it continued uninterruptedly in the years that followed (Freire 1983: ix–x).

10. For a critical analysis of Entwistle's interpretation of Gramsci's pedagogical ideas, see Giroux 1988: 196–203.

11. Later, Freire referred to reactions from executives in education and teachers against the participation of the lower social classes in the operation of schools in São Paulo. He attributed these reactions to the elitist-authoritarian ideology that they had adopted (Freire 1999b: 90).

12. For the authoritarian political practice of these forces in the educational sector, see Borg and Mayo 2000: 106.

13. According to a report, the ideas behind the reform in São Paulo were popular in other Brazilian cities, Porto Alegre being one of them. If we glance through the relevant literature, we can see that Freire's influence on school democratization in that municipality is quite evident (Mayo 2004: 91–92).

14. Considerable criticism has been exercised against Freire's sexist language. Freire accepted this kind of criticism despite the fact that it lacked understanding of his own history of ideological and political formation (Freire and Macedo 1993: 170–176). Of course, not all feminists agreed with hooks's view, which characterized all feminists who supported this kind of criticism as privileged academics (hooks 1993: 146–149). She did not underestimate Freire's contribution, which she compared to water that thirsty people crave even though there is some dirt in it. Furthermore, according to Darder, in addition to feminists, Freire's work was subjected to criticism in the United States by Marxists because it did not offer a systematic analysis of social classes, capitalism, and schools, and by African American researchers because it lacked a profound and detailed knowledge of the historical formation of racism in that country (Darder 2002: 43).

15. According to Kincheloe, during discussion with him, Freire expressed his anger at those who call themselves Freireans and who entered their classrooms with nothing to teach, claiming that it would be an act of violence to bring a body of knowledge into the classroom, yet at the same time invited their students to produce this knowledge (Kincheloe and Steinberg 2002: 24).

NOTES TO CHAPTER 4

1. The text "Education, Liberation, and the Church," written in 1973 and included in *The Politics of Education,* illustrates this (Freire 1985a: 121–142). According to an interpretation by Johns, Freire followed Marx's basic position (which considered religion as people's creation, a product of alienation) as well as maintaining that religion was a reflection of one's sociopolitical status and that the three types of churches (traditional, modern, and prophetic) in Latin America represented three different types of political thought and were associated with class struggle (Johns 1998: 103).

2. For a comparison of Dewey's problem solving and Freire's problem posing, see Streck 1977: 127–134.

3. Saviani was a Brazilian professor critical of Freire's pedagogy (see Chapter 3).

4. See Schubert et al. 2002: 7.

5. See Urban and Wagoner 2000: 201–202; Gonzalez 1986: 28–29, 53–67.

6. See Kliebard 1995: 78–85, 90, 99, 194; Kliebard, 1999: 49; Marsh and Willis 2003: 43–44.

7. See Kliebard 1995: 35–44; Pinar et al. 2002: 83–87; Counts 1978: 3–7, 25–28, 33–44.

8. For more details on Dewey's perspective, see Carr and Hartnett 1997: 60; Karier 1973: 97–99, 104–106; Karier 2002: 85–86; Archambault 1965: vi; Mayhew and Edwards 1965: viii, ix, xiii, 4, 20, 23, 36, 40–41; Schutz 2001: 273–279; Jackson 1990: xxix–xxx.

9. As Torres stresses, critical pedagogy has been inspired by Freire as well as by a critical reading of Dewey's work (Torres 1998: 245).

10. As regards curriculum planning in the social reconstruction perspective, see Kliebard 1995: 21–25, 158–162, 171–175; Kliebard 2002: 64–65; Counts 1978: 3–7, 25–28, 33–44; Brameld 1956: vi–vii, 4–5, 31, 160, 166–167, 170, 197–199, 211.

11. This point is stressed by Allman 2001: 196.

12. See Shor 1992: 119–122; Beane 1990: 37–38: Pinar et al. 2002: 661–699; Schubert et al. 2002: 261, 382–391.

13. See Noutsos 1983: 43–55.

14. See Rasis 2004: 360–363.

15. See Flouris 2000: 28; Bruner 1960: 26–29; Kliebard 1995: 228–230: Pinar 2004: 7.

16. See Posner 2004: 24–26; Heimariou 1987: 84–85.

17. See Posner 2004: 61–63.

18. For more details on the reconceptualization of the curriculum field, see Apple 1993: 15–23; Apple 2001: 47–89; Pinar et al. 2002: 159–239; Schubert et al. 2002: 193–195; Pinar 2004: 72; Marsh and Willis 2003: 249–252.

19. See Teitelbaum 1998: 34–36, 40–51.

20. See Marshall, Sears, and Schubert 2000: 161–162.

BIBLIOGRAPHY

Alexander, R. 1962. *Labor Relations in Argentina, Brazil, and Chile.* New York: McGraw-Hill.
———. 1999. *International Maoism in the Developing World.* Westport, CT: Praeger.
Allman, P. 1994. "Paulo Freire's Contributions to Radical Adult Education." *Studies in the Education of Adults* 26, no. 2: 144–161.
———. 1997. "Commentary: Paulo Freire and the Future of the Radical Tradition." *Studies in the Education of Adults* 29, no. 2: 113–120.
———. 2001. *Critical Education Against Global Capitalism: Karl Marx and Revolutionary Critical Education.* Westport, CT: Bergin and Garvey.
Apple, M. 1993. *Official Knowledge: Democratic Education in a Conservative Age.* New York: Routledge.
———. 2001. *Eksinhronismos kai sintiritismos stin ekpaidefsi* [Modernization and conservatism in education]. Athens: Metaihmio.
Araujo, M. 1998. "Notes." In *Pedagogy of the Heart,* by P. Freire, 109–141. New York: Continuum.
———. 1999. "Notes." In *Pedagogy of Hope: Reliving Pedagogy of the Oppressed,* by P. Freire, 205–240. New York: Continuum.
———. 2001. *Chronicles of Love: My Life with Paulo Freire.* New York: Peter Lang.
Araujo, M., and D. Macedo. 1998. "Introduction." In *The Paulo Freire Reader,* edited by M. Araujo and D. Macedo, 1–44. New York: Continuum.
Archambault, R. 1965. "Editor's Foreword." In *The Dewey School: The Laboratory School of the University of Chicago, 1896–1903,* by K. Mayhew and A. Edwards, v–vi. New York: Atherton Press.

Aronowitz, S. 1993. "Paulo Freire's Radical Democratic Humanism." In *Paulo Freire: A Critical Encounter,* edited by P. McLaren and P. Leonard, 8–24. London: Routledge.

Austin, R. 1997. "Freire, Frei, and Literary Texts in Chile, 1964–1970." In *Latin American Education: Comparative Perspectives,* edited by C. A. Torres and A. Puiggros, 323–348. Boulder, CO: Westview Press.

Baiocchi, G. 2003. "Radicals in Power." In *Radicals in Power: The Workers Party (PT) and Experiments in Urban Democracy in Brazil,* edited by G. Baiocchi, 1–26. London: Zed Books.

Barnard, C. 1980. "Imperialism, Underdevelopment, and Education." In *Literacy and Revolution: The Pedagogy of Paulo Freire,* edited by R. Mackie, 15–35. London: Pluto Press.

Beane, J. 1990. *Affect in the Curriculum: Toward Democracy, Dignity, and Diversity.* New York: Teachers College Press.

Borg, C., and P. Mayo. 2000. "Reflections from a 'Third Age' Marriage: Paulo Freire's Pedagogy of Reason, Hope, and Passion. An Interview with Ana Maria (Nita) Freire." *McGill Journal of Education* 35, no. 2: 105–120.

Brameld, T. 1956. *Toward a Reconstructed Philosophy of Education.* New York: Dryden Press.

Branford, S. 2003. "The Making of a Leader." In *Lula and the Workers Party in Brazil,* by S. Branford, B. Kucinski, and H. Wainright, 63–79. New York: New Press.

Brown, C. 1987. "Literacy in 30 Hours: Paulo Freire's Process in Northeast Brazil." In *Freire for the Classroom: A Sourcebook for Liberatory Teaching,* edited by I. Shor, 215–231. Portsmouth, NH: Boynton/Cook.

Bruneau, T. 1974. *Political Transformation of the Brazilian Catholic Church.* London: Cambridge University Press.

Bruner, J. 1960. *I diadikasia tis paideias* [The process of education]. Athens: Karavias.

Carmen, R. 1998. "Paulo Freire 1921—1997: A Philosophy of Hope, a Life of Practice." *Development on Practice* 8, no. 1: 64–67.

Carr, W., and A. Hartnett. 1997. *Education and the Struggle for Democracy: The Politics of Educational Ideas.* Buckingham, UK: Open University Press.

Coben, D. 1998. *Radical Heroes: Gramsci, Freire, and the Politics of Adult Education.* New York: Garland.

Coletti, L. 1982. *Oi ideologies apo to 68 mehri simera* [Ideologies from 1968 until today]. Athens: Odysseas.

Collins, D. 1973. "Two Utopians: A Comparison and Contrast of the Educational Philosophies of Paulo Freire and Theodore Brameld." Ph.D. diss., University of Southern California.

Counts, G. 1978. *Dare the School Build a New Social Order?* Carbondale: Southern Illinois University Press.

Crawford, L. 1980. "Comparative Education." *Educational Studies* 11, no. 1: 67–68.

Darcy de Oliveira, R., and M. Darcy de Oliveira. 1976. *IDAC Document 11/12*. Geneva: Institute for Cultural Action.

Darder, A. 2002. *Reinventing Paulo Freire: A Pedagogy of Love*. Boulder, CO: Westview Press.

Elias, J. 1973. "Adult Literacy Education in Brazil, 1961–1964: Metodo Paulo Freire." *Canadian and International Education* 2, no. 1: 67–84.

―――. 1994. *Paulo Freire: Pedagogue of Liberation*. Malabar, FL: Krieger.

Evans, D. 1986. "Mi typiki ekpaidefsi: Oi piges kai oi simasies tis [Non-formal education: Its sources and meanings]." In *Gia mia laiki paideia: Enallaktikoi thesmoi kai politikes* [For an education of the masses: Alternative institutions and policies], edited by Kentro Meleton kai Aftomorfosis; translated by M. Katsoulis, 105–123. Athens: Geniki Grammateia Laikis Epimorfosis.

Facundo, B. 1984. *Freire-Inspired Programs in the United States and Puerto Rico: A Critical Evaluation*. Washington, DC: Latino Institute. http://nlu.nl.edu/ace/Resources/Documents/Facundo.html (accessed January 19, 2001).

Findlay, P. 1994. "Conscientization and Social Movements in Canada: The Relevance of Paulo Freire's Ideas in Contemporary Politics." In *Politics of Liberation: Paths from Freire*, edited by P. McLaren and C. Lankshear, 108–122. London: Routledge.

Flouris, G. 2000. *Analytika programmata gia mia nea epohi stin ekpaidefsi* [Curricula for a new era in education]. Athens: Grigoris.

Frank, A. 1969. *Latin America: Underdevelopment or Revolution*. New York: Monthly Review Press.

―――. 1972. "Capitalist Underdevelopment or Socialist Revolution?" In *Latin America: The Dynamics of Social Change*, edited by S. Halper and J. Sterling, 140–162. New York: St. Martin's Press and Monthly Review Press.

Frankenstein, M. 1997. "Breaking Down the Dichotomy Between Learning and Teaching Mathematics." In *Mentoring the Mentor: A Critical Dialogue with Paulo Freire*, edited by P. Freire, J. Fraser, D. Macedo, T. McKinnon, and W. Stokes, 59–87. New York: Peter Lang.

Frankenstein, M., and A. Powell. 1994. "Toward Liberatory Mathematics: Paulo Freire's Epistemology and Ethnomathematics." In *Politics of Liberation: Paths from Freire*, edited by P. McLaren and C. Lankshear, 74–99. London: Routledge.

Freire, P. 1972. "Education: Domestication or Liberation?" *Prospects* 2: 173–181.

―――. 1973. "A Few Notions About the Word Conscientization." *Hard Cheese*, no. 1: 23–28.

———. 1974. "Education as the Practice of Freedom." In *Education: The Practice of Freedom*, by P. Freire, 3–84. London: Writers and Readers Publishing Cooperative.

———. 1976. "Are Adult Literacy Programmes Neutral?" In *A Turning Point for Literacy: Adult Education for Development—the Spirit and Declaration of Persepolis*, edited by L. Bataille, 195–200. Oxford, UK: Pergamon Press.

———. 1978. *Pedagogy in Process: The Letters to Guinea-Bissau*. London: Writers and Readers Publishing Cooperative.

———. 1981. "The People Speak Their Word: Learning to Read and Write in São Tomé and Principe." *Harvard Educational Review* 51, no. 1: 27–45.

———. 1983. "Foreword." In *Theory and Resistance in Education: A Pedagogy for the Opposition*, by H. Giroux, ix–x. London: Heinemann Educational Books.

———. 1985a. *The Politics of Education: Culture, Power, and Liberation*. Westport, CT: Bergin and Garvey.

———. 1985b. "Reading the World and the Word: An Interview with Paulo Freire." *Language Arts* 62, no. 1: 12–20.

———. 1987. "Letter to North American Teachers." In *Freire for the Classroom: A Sourcebook for Liberatory Teaching*, edited by I. Shor, 211–214. Portsmouth, NH: Boynton/Cook.

———. 1991. "The Importance of the Act of the Reading." In *Rewriting Literacy: Culture and the Discourse of the Other*, edited by C. Mitchell and K. Weiler, 139–145. New York: Bergin and Garvey.

———. 1993a. *Pedagogy of the City*. New York: Continuum.

———. 1993b. *Pedagogy of the Heart*. New York: Continuum.

———. 1995. "Reply to Discussants." In *Paulo Freire at the Institute*, edited by M. de Figueiredo-Cowen and D. Gastaldo, 61–67. London: University of London Institute of Education.

———. 1996a. *Letters to Christina: Reflections on My Life and Work*. New York: Routledge.

———. 1996b. *Pedagogy of the Oppressed*, translated by M. Bergman Ramos. London: Penguin.

———. 1997. "A Response." In *Mentoring the Mentor: A Critical Dialogue with Paulo Freire*, edited by P. Freire, J. Fraser, D. Macedo, T. McKinnon, and W. Stokes, 303–329. New York: Peter Lang.

———. 1998a. *Pedagogy of Freedom: Ethics, Democracy, and Civic Courage*. Lanham, MD: Rowman and Littlefield.

———. 1998b. *Politics and Education*. Los Angeles: University of California Latin American Center Publications.

———. 1998c. *Teachers as Cultural Workers: Letters to Those Who Dare Teach*. Boulder, CO: Westview Press.

Bibliography

———. 1999a. "Education and Community Involvement." In *Critical Education in the New Information Age*, by M. Castells, R. Flencha, P. Freire, H. Giroux, D. Macedo, and P. Willis, 83–91. Lanham: MD: Rowman and Littlefield.

———. 1999b. *Pedagogy of Hope: Reliving Pedagogy of the Oppressed.* New York: Continuum.

———. 2004. *Pedagogy of Indignation.* Boulder, CO: Paradigm Publishers.

Freire, P., and A. Faundez. 1992. *Learning to Question: A Pedagogy of Liberation.* New York: Continuum.

Freire, P., and M. Gadotti. 1995. "We Can Reinvent the World." In *Critical Theory and Educational Research,* edited by P. McLaren and J. Giarelli, 257–270. Albany, NY: State University of New York Press.

Freire, P., and D. Macedo. 1987. *Literacy: Reading the Word and the World.* Westport, CT: Bergin and Garvey.

———. 1993. "A Dialogue with Paulo Freire." In *Paulo Freire: A Critical Encounter,* edited by P. McLaren and P. Leonard, 169–176. London: Routledge.

———. 1995. "A Dialogue: Culture, Language, and Race." *Harvard Educational Review* 65, no. 3: 377–402.

French, J. 1992. *The Brazilian Worker's ABC: Class Conflict and Alliances in Modern São Paulo.* Chapel Hill: University of North Carolina Press.

Gadotti, M. 1994. *Reading Paulo Freire: His Life and Work.* Albany: State University of New York Press.

———. 1997. "Contemporary Brazilian Education: Challenges of Basic Education." In *Latin American Education: Comparative Perspectives,* edited by C. A. Torres and A. Puiggros, 123–148. Boulder, CO: Westview Press.

Galenson, W. 1962. *Labor in Developing Economies.* Berkeley and Los Angeles: University of California Press.

Galli, R., and J. Jones. 1987. *Guinea-Bissau: Politics, Economics, and Society.* London: Frances Pinter.

Gibson, R. 1994. "The Promethean Literacy: Paulo Freire's Pedagogy of Reading, Praxis, and Liberation." Ph.D. diss., Pennsylvania State University.

Giroux, H. 1981. *Ideology, Culture, and the Process of Schooling.* London: Falmer Press.

———. 1988. *Teachers as Intellectuals: Toward a Critical Pedagogy of Learning.* New York: Bergin and Garvey.

Giroux, H., and P. McLaren. 1994. *Paulo Freire on Higher Education: A Dialogue at the National University of Mexico.* Albany: State University of New York Press.

Gleeson, D. 1974. "'Theory' and 'Practice' in the Sociology of Paulo Freire." *Hard Cheese,* no. 3: 28–38.

Gonzalez, G. 1986. *Progressive Education: A Marxist Interpretation*. Minneapolis: Marxist Educational Press.

Goulet, D. 1974. "Introduction." In *Education: The Practice of Freedom*, by P. Freire, vii–xiv. London: Writers and Readers Publishing Cooperative.

Grollios, G., R. Karandaidou, D. Korombokis, Ch. Kotinis, and T. Liambas. 2002. *Grammatismos kai siniditopiisi: Mia pedagogiki prosegisi me vasi ti theoria tou Paulo Freire* [Literacy and conscientization: A pedagogical approach based on Paulo Freire's theory]. Athens: Metaihmio.

Hall, M., and M. Garcia. 1989. "Urban Labor." In *Modern Brazil: Elites and Masses in Historical Perspective*, edited by M. Conniff and F. McCann, 163–195. Lincoln: University of Nebraska Press.

Heimariou, E. 1987. *Analytika programmata: Sinhrones taseis sxediasmou stin Anglia* [Curricula: Modern trends in planning in England]. Thessaloniki, Greece: Kyriakidis.

hooks, b. 1993. "bell hooks Speaking About Paulo Freire—the Man, His Work." In *Paulo Freire: A Critical Encounter*, edited by P. McLaren and P. Leonard, 146–154. London: Routledge.

Horton, M., and P. Freire. 1990. *We Make the Road by Walking: Conversations on Education and Social Change*, edited by B. Bell, J. Gavenda, and J. Peters. Philadelphia: Temple University Press.

Ireland, T. 1987. *Antonio Gramsci and Adult Education: Reflections on the Brazilian Experience*. Manchester Monographs. University of Manchester Centre for Adult and Higher Education. Manchester, UK: University of Manchester Press.

Jackson, P. 1990. "Introduction." In *The School and Society and the Child and the Curriculum*, by J. Dewey, ix–xxxvii. Chicago: University of Chicago Press.

Jaguaribe, H. 1972. "The Brazilian Structural Crisis." In *Latin America: The Dynamics of Social Change*, edited by S. Halper and J. Sterling, 35–56. New York: St. Martin's Press.

Jarvis, P. 1987. "Paulo Freire." In *Twentieth-Century Thinkers in Adult Education*, edited by P. Jarvis, 265–279. New York: Croom Helm.

Jevez, C., and J. Hernandez-Pico. 1973. "Controversy." *Convergence* 6, no. 1: 8.

Jeria, J. 1986. "Vagabond of the Obvious: The Life and Writings of Paulo Freire." *Vitae Scholasticae* 5, nos. 1–2: 1–59.

Johns, C. 1998. *Pentecostal Formation: A Pedagogy Among the Oppressed*. Sheffield, UK: Sheffield Academic Press.

Kane, L. 2000. "Popular Education and the Landless People's Movement in Brazil." *Studies in the Education of Adults* 32, no. 1: 36–49.

Karier, C. 1973. "Liberal Ideology and the Quest for Orderly Change." In *Roots of Crisis: American Education in the Twentieth Century*, edited by C. Karier, P. Violas, and J. Spring, 84–107. Chicago: Rand McNally.

————. 2002. "The Quest for Orderly Change: Some Reflections." In *History of Education: Major Themes*. Vol. 1, *Debates in the History of Education*, edited by R. Lowe, 74–90. London: Routledge.

Kennedy, W. 1981. "Highlander Praxis: Learning with Myles and Horton." *Teachers College Record* 83, no. 1: 105–119.

Kincheloe, J., and S. Steinberg. 2002. "A Legacy of Paulo Freire: A Conversation." In *The Freirean Legacy: Educating for Social Justice*, edited by J. Slater, S. Fain, and C. Rossato, 15–26. New York: Peter Lang.

Kirkwood, G., and C. Kirkwood. 1989. *Living Adult Education: Freire in Scotland*. Philadelphia: Open University Press.

Kliebard, H. 1995. *The Struggle for the American Curriculum, 1893–1958*. New York: Routledge.

————. 1999. *Schooled to Work: Vocationalism and the American Curriculum, 1876–1946*. New York: Teachers College Press.

————. 2002. *Changing Course: American Curriculum Reform in the Twentieth Century*. New York: Teachers College Press.

Kucinski, B. 2003. "The Rise of the Workers Party." In *Lula and the Workers Party in Brazil*, by S. Bradford, B. Kucinski, and H. Wainwright, 23–62. London: New Press.

La Belle, T. 1976. "Goals and Strategies of Nonformal Education in Latin America." *Comparative Education Review* (October): 328–345.

Leistyna, P. 2004. "Presence of Mind in the Process of Learning and Knowing: A Dialogue with Paulo Freire." *Teacher Education Quarterly* 31, no. 1: 17–29.

Leonard, S. 1990. *Critical Theory in Political Practice*. Princeton, NJ: Princeton University Press.

Macedo, D. 1991. "The Politics of an Emancipatory Literacy in Cape Verde." In *Rewriting Literacy: Culture and the Discourse of the Other*, edited by C. Mitchell and K. Weiler, 147–159. New York: Bergin and Garvey.

————. 2001. "Introduction." In *Chronicles of Love: My Life with Paulo Freire*, by M. Araujo, 1–9. New York: Peter Lang.

Malcolm, L. 1999. "Mortimer Adler, Paulo Freire, and Teaching Theology in a Democracy." *Teaching Theology and Religion* 2, no. 2: 80–95.

Marsh, C., and G. Willis. 2003. *Curriculum: Alternative Approaches, Ongoing Issues*. New Jersey: Merril Prentice Hall.

Marshall, D., J. Sears, and W. Schubert. 2000. *Turning Points in Curriculum: A Contemporary American Memoir*. Englewood Cliffs, NJ: Prentice Hall.

Mathew, G. 1980. *A Day with Paulo Freire*. New Delhi: Indian Society for Promoting Christian Knowledge.

Matthews, M. 1980. "Knowledge, Action, and Power." In *Literacy and Revolution: The Pedagogy of Paulo Freire*, edited by R. Mackie, 81–105. London: Pluto Press.

Mayhew, K., and A. Edwards. 1965. *The Dewey School: The Laboratory School of the University of Chicago, 1896–1903.* New York: Atherton Press.

Mayo, P. 1994. "Synthesizing Gramsci and Freire: Possibilities for a Theory of Radical Adult Education." *International Journal of Lifelong Education* 13, no. 2: 134–142.

———. 1996. "Transformative Adult Education in an Age of Globalisation: A Gramscian-Freirean Synthesis and Beyond." *Alberta Journal of Educational Research* 42, no. 2: 148–160.

———. 1997. "Paulo Freire, 1921–1997: An Appreciation." *Convergence* 30, no. 1: 4–8.

———. 1999. *Gramsci, Freire, and Adult Education: Possibilities for Transformative Action.* London: Zed Books.

———. 2004. *Liberating Praxis, Paulo Freire's Legacy for Radical Education, and Politics.* Westport, CT: Praeger.

McLaren, P. 1988. "Foreword." In *Teachers as Intellectuals: Toward a Critical Pedagogy of Learning,* by H. Giroux, ix–xxi. New York: Bergin and Garvey.

———. 2000. *Che Guevara, Paulo Freire, and the Pedagogy of Revolution.* Lanham, MD: Rowman and Littlefield.

McLaren, P., and C. Lankshear. 1994. "Introduction." In *Politics of Liberation: Paths from Freire,* edited by P. McLaren, and C. Lankshear, 1–11. London: Routledge.

Milios, G. 1997. *Theories gia ton pagkosmio kapitalismo* [Theories on global capitalism]. Athens: Kritiki.

Morray, J. 1968. "The United States and Latin America." In *Latin America: Reform or Revolution—a Reader,* edited by J. Petras and M. Zeitlin, 95–109. New York: Fawcett.

Noutsos, M. 1983. *Didaktikoi stohoi kai analytiko programma: Kritiki mias synhronis paidagogikis ideologias* [Educational objectives and the curriculum: Criticism of a modern pedagogical ideology]. Ioannina, Greece: Dodoni.

Nylen, W. 2000. "The Making of a Loyal Opposition: The Workers' Party (PT) and the Consolidation of Democracy in Brazil." In *Democratic Brazil: Actors, Institutions, and Processes,* edited by P. Kingstone and T. Power, 126–143. Pittsburgh: University of Pittsburgh Press.

O'Cadiz, M.D.P., P. L. Wong, and C. A. Torres. 1998. *Education and Democracy: Paulo Freire, Social Movements, and Educational Reform in São Paulo.* Boulder, CO: Westview Press.

O'Gorman, F. 1978. "Conscientization—Whose Initiative Should It Be?" *Convergence* 11, no. 1: 32–59.

Oldenski, T. 1997. *Liberation Theology and Critical Pedagogy in Today's Catholic Schools: Social Justice in Action.* New York: Garland.

Owensby, B. 1999. *Initiative Ironies: Modernity and the Making of Middle-Class Lives in Brazil.* Palo Alto, CA: Stanford University Press.

Bibliography

Pereira, A. 1997. "The Crisis of Developmentalism and the Rural Labor Movement in North-East Brazil." In *The New Politics of Inequality in Latin America: Rethinking Participation and Representation*, edited by D. Chambers, K. Hite, S. Martin, K. Piester, M. Seggara, and C. Vilas, 95–112. Oxford, UK: Oxford University Press.

Pinar, W. 2004. *What Is Curriculum Theory?* Mahwah, NJ: Lawrence Erlbaum.

Pinar, W., W. Reynolds, P. Slattery, and P. Taubman. 2002. *Understanding Curriculum: An Introduction to the Study of Historical and Contemporary Curriculum Discourses*. New York: Peter Lang.

Posner, G. 2004. *Analyzing the Curriculum*. New York: McGraw–Hill.

Puiggros, A. 1994. "Politics, Praxis, and the Personal: An Argentine Assessment." In *Politics of Liberation: Paths from Freire*, edited by P. McLaren and C. Lankshear, 154–172. London: Routledge.

Rasis, S. 2004. *Ta panepistimia htes kai simera: Symvoli stin istoria tis ekpaidefsis—i Agglosaxoniki empeiria* [Universities in the past and the present: Contribution to the history of education—the Anglo-Saxon experience]. Athens: Papazisis.

Reese, W. 2000. "Grassroots Movements During the Progressive Era." In *History of Education: Major Themes*. Vol. 3, *Studies in Learning and Teaching*, edited by R. Lowe, 270–286. London: Routledge.

Rivera, R. 2004. *A Study of Liberation Discourse: The Semantics of Opposition in Freire and Gutierrez*. New York: Peter Lang.

Roberts, P. 2000. *Education, Literacy, and Humanization: Exploring the Work of Paulo Freire*. Westport, CT: Bergin and Garvey.

Rossato, C. 2002. "Critical Pedagogy, Applied Praxis: A Freirean Interdisciplinary Project and Grassroot Social Movement." In *The Freirean Legacy: Educating for Social Justice*, edited by J. Slater, S. Fain, and C. Rossato, 157–171. New York: Peter Lang.

———. 2005. *Engaging Paulo Freire's Pedagogy of Possibility: From Blind to Transformative Optimism*. Lanham, MD: Rowman and Littlefield.

Saul, A. M. 1993. "São Paulo's Education Revisited." Postscript in *Pedagogy of the City*, by P. Freire, 145–165. New York: Continuum.

Schipani, D. 1984. *Conscientization and Creativity: Paulo Freire and Christian Education*. Lanham, MD: University Press of America.

Schubert, W., A. Schubert, T. Thomas, and W. Carrol. 2002. *Curriculum Books: The First Hundred Years*. New York: Peter Lang.

Schugurensky, D. 1998. "The Legacy of Paulo Freire: A Critical Review of His Contributions." *Convergence* 31, nos. 1–2: 17–28.

Schutz, A. 2001. "John Dewey's Conundrum: Can Democratic Schools Empower?" *Teachers College Record* 103, no. 2: 260–281.

Shor, I. 1992. *Culture Wars: School and Society in the Conservative Restoration*. Chicago: University of Chicago Press.

Shor, I., and P. Freire. 1987. *A Pedagogy for Liberation: Dialogues on Transforming Education.* Westport, CT: Bergin and Garvey.

Sieber, T. 1997. "Pedagogy, Power, and the City: Paulo Freire as Urban School Superintendent." In *Mentoring the Mentor: A Critical Dialogue with Paulo Freire,* edited by P. Freire, J. Fraser, D. Macedo, T. McKinnon, and W. Stokes, 237–282. New York: Peter Lang.

Stefanos, A. 1997. "African Women and Revolutionary Change: A Freirian and Feminist Perspective." In *Mentoring the Mentor: A Critical Dialogue with Paulo Freire,* edited by P. Freire, J. Fraser, D. Macedo, T. McKinnon, and W. Stokes, 243–271. New York: Peter Lang.

Streck, D. 1977. "John Dewey's and Paulo Freire's Views on the Political Function of Education, with Special Emphasis on the Problem of Method." Ph.D. diss., Rutgers University.

Tadeu da Silva, T., and P. McLaren. 1993. "Knowledge Under Siege: The Brazilian Debate." In *Paulo Freire: A Critical Encounter,* edited by P. McLaren and P. Leonard, 36–46. London: Routledge.

Teitelbaum, K. 1998. "Contestation and Curriculum: The Efforts of American Socialists, 1900–1920." In *The Curriculum: Problems, Politics, and Possibilities,* edited by L. Beyer and M. Apple, 30–55. Albany: State University of New York Press.

Torres, C. A. 1993. "From the Pedagogy of the Oppressed to a Luta Continua: The Political Pedagogy of Paulo Freire." In *Paulo Freire: A Critical Encounter,* edited by P. McLaren and P. Leonard, 119–145. London: Routledge.

Torres, C. A. 1994a. "Foreword: A Land of Contrasts and a Pedagogy of Contradiction." In *Reading Paulo Freire: His Life and Work,* edited by M. Gadotti, ix–xii. Albany: State University of New York Press.

———. 1994b. "Paulo Freire as Secretary of Education in the Municipality of São Paulo." *Comparative Education Review* 38, no. 2: 181–214.

———. 1998. *Education, Power, and Personal Biography: Dialogues with Critical Educators.* London: Routledge.

Torres, C. A. and Freire, P. 1994. "Twenty Years After *Pedagogy of the Oppressed*: Paulo Freire in Conversation with Carlos Alberto Torres." In *Politics of Liberation: Paths from Freire,* edited by P. McLaren and C. Lankshear, 100–107. London: Routledge.

Urban, W., and J. Wagoner. 2000. *American Education: A History.* Boston: McGraw-Hill.

Van Vugt, J. 1991. *Democratic Organization for Social Change: Latin American Christian Base Communities and Literacy Campaigns.* New York: Bergin and Garvey.

Walker, J. 1980. "The End of Dialogue: Paulo Freire on Politics and Education." In *Literacy and Revolution: The Pedagogy of Paulo Freire,* edited by R. Mackie, 125–143. London: Pluto Press.

Weiler, K. 1991. "Freire and a Feminist Pedagogy of Difference." *Harvard Educational Review* 61, no. 4: 449–474.

Weinstein, B. 1996. *The Social Peace in Brazil: Industrialists and the Remaking of the Working Class in São Paulo, 1920–1964.* Chapel Hill: University of North Carolina Press.

Wong, P. L. 1995. "Constructing a Public Popular Education in São Paulo." *Comparative Education Review* 39, no. 1: 120–141.

Wright, A., and W. Wolford. 2003. *To Inherit the Earth: The Landless Movement and the Struggle for a New Brazil.* Oakland, CA: Food First Books.

INDEX

Index

Mannheim, Karl, 22, 148
Mao Zedong, 46, 48–49, 51, 60, 66, 82, 118, 127
Marcuse, Herbert, 3, 46
Maritain, Jacques, 14
Marx, Karl, 21, 47–49, 60, 63, 91, 106, 120–121, 149–152
Marxism: 21, 42, 46–47, 50, 65, 81–82, 93, 105, 119–120, 125, 132, 141; -Leninism, 21, 46
Marxist, 3, 27, 46–47, 50–51, 60, 65, 76, 81, 106, 116, 119–121, 126, 145, 149–150, 152
Medellín General Conference of the Latin American Episcopate, 44, 148
Mexico, 1, 5, 53, 149
Miskitos, 82–83
Mississippi Freedom School, 142
Monthly Review, 46, 91
Mounier, Emanuel, 14, 21, 31
Movement for Popular Culture (MCP), 19, 23–25, 27, 37, 112–113
Movement for the Education of the Base (MEB), 21–22, 27, 112
Movement for Unified Popular Action, 43

National Confederation of Catholic Workers, 15
National Confederation of Industrial Workers, 19
National Confederation of Peasant Laborers, 28
National Confederation of Rural Workers, 20
National Conference of Bishops of Brazil, 27
National Service for Industrial Training, 15
nationalism(s), 5, 17, 24, 38, 112
Neo-Marxist, 21, 81

New School, 34–35, 111–115, 121
New State of Brazil, 15
Nicaragua, 82

oppressed: 33, 50, 52, 61, 85, 88, 92, 107–110, 117, 126, 151; binary opposition of oppressors/, 119; classes, 96, 119; liberator of the, 49; oppressors and the, 50; pedagogy of the, 3; as a social class, 51; struggles of the, 121
Oswaldo Cruz School, 13, 14

Peasant Leagues (LC), 19–21, 112
Perdosa, Mário, 75
Pernambuco, 11, 15–18, 20, 25–26
Perón, Juan, 15, 42
Persepolis, 56
Piaget, Jean, 140
Pinto, Ronaldo, 44
Pluralism, 15, 77, 93–94
politics: 49, 72, 89; Brazilian, 74; education and, 42, 88, 102
Pope John XXIII, 21, 148
Popular Action (AP), 20–21, 112
Popular Action Front (FRAP), 43
Populism, 15
Portuguese, 14–15, 29, 54–56, 99, 147–149
Positivism, 93, 150
Postliteracy, 40, 72, 115
Pracinhas da FEB school, 100

Quadros, Janio, 22–23, 25

radicalization: 30, 112; in the Brazilian Catholic Church, 21; of the Brazilian popular social classes, 19, 23; of the lower social classes, 19, 112; of the masses, 113, 116; of the working classes, 112

ABOUT THE AUTHOR

George Grollios is Associate Professor of Pedagogy and Curriculum in the Department of Primary Education at Aristotle University of Thessaloniki, Greece. His many publications include a previous book about literacy and Paulo Freire.